GARDEN PLANTS

...IN COLOR

Edited by HENRY T. SKINNER

GARDEN PLANTS

...IN COLOR

Edited by HENRY T. SKINNER

VOLUME 1

Trees

Shrubs

Vines

First Edition

Published by SWEENEY, KRIST AND DIMM *Portland 9, Oregon, U.S.A.*

1958

First Edition, November 1958

GARDEN PLANTS IN COLOR

VOLUME 1

Trees

Shrubs

Vines

LIBRARY OF CONGRESS CARD CATALOG NUMBER 58-59510

© *Copyright 1958 by*

SWEENEY, KRIST AND DIMM

HORTICULTURAL PRINTERS AND PUBLISHERS

535 NORTHWEST SIXTEENTH AVE., PORTLAND 9, OREGON

DISTRIBUTED BY

DODD, MEAD & COMPANY - NEW YORK

Manufactured in the United States of America

Preface

FOR MANY YEARS there has been a need within the nursery industry for an authoritative publication devoted to a presentation of color plates of ornamental plants generally available in the commercial nurseries of the country. "GARDEN PLANTS IN COLOR" meets this need.

In the past, several of the larger wholesale nurseries have made valuable contributions to horticultural literature by publishing books on their specialties; they have used color extensively. Others have issued collections of color plates devoted to specific groups of plants such as roses and shrubs. Some publishers have entered this field with popular publications on garden plants in which color is used primarily to make the publication attractive to the amateur gardener.

"GARDEN PLANTS IN COLOR," on the contrary, has as its objective the presentation of concise descriptions of over 400 nursery items, generally available in the trade, each of which is illustrated in full color. The accuracy of the descriptions is attested to by the fact that they have been edited in detail by Dr. Henry T. Skinner, Director of the United States National Arboretum. The color work is the result of excellent original photographs plus a superb and painstaking job of reproduction. The combination of the best of raw materials and the expert craftsmanship in production has produced a classic and valuable contribution to horticultural literature.

"GARDEN PLANTS IN COLOR" will render a long-needed service to the nursery industry, for even though it was physically impossible to illustrate all of the thousands of plants that nurserymen grow, it does cover those plants which are generally available and which constitute a high proportion of the total volume of the industry.

Each of the eight sections is introduced by a brief description of the group, written by recognized plantsmen, six of whom were drawn from the nursery industry itself, one from an arboretum, and one from an outstanding public park. This in itself is unique, and is indicative of the publisher's insistence that this presentation be of the greatest practical value possible.

"GARDEN PLANTS IN COLOR" is the first attempt to cover the horticultural industry of the United States in such a comprehensive manner and the publishers are to be commended for the effort. Due to practical limitations, however, complete coverage between the covers of a single book could not be accomplished. The omission of Roses will be questioned. But owing to the comparative rapidity of change now going on from many of the older sorts of roses to the newer improved varieties, the decision to omit the class entirely at this time was well taken. A supplement to "GARDEN PLANTS IN COLOR" should be devoted to this one popular plant. On the other hand, the decision to include Rhododendrons, Azaleas and Camellias was a sound one, as here will be found in one place and for the first time, full color illustrations of 150 popular varieties of these plants.

"GARDEN PLANTS IN COLOR" is not a static thing, therefore; it is a living volume of the best in ornamental horticulture today which will grow into the best of tomorrow.

RICHARD P. WHITE

Washington, D.C.
September 1958

Foreword

NURSERYMEN IN MANY sections of the United States have indicated their need for a book illustrating in color the plants that they grow and sell. The publishers have created "GARDEN PLANTS IN COLOR" to fill this need. Once it was decided to publish an illustrated volume, the big question arose: "What should be illustrated?" The first impulse was to use just those illustrations of trees, shrubs, and vines available in the publisher's library. After thorough exploration into the subject, it was evident that in order to serve the maximum horticultural industry a wider range of plants must be included.

At this point, the staff of "GARDEN PLANTS IN COLOR" decided to have experienced nurserymen, landscape architects, and horticultural scientists help answer the question, "What to illustrate." Check lists of plants in each of the eight classifications to be illustrated were sent to experienced horticulturists throughout the country. They were asked to select the varieties best for their locality and add other important varieties not included on the original lists. As those check lists were returned, they were combined into a single list of the most popular plants. Guided by this list of favorites, selections were made of the suitable subjects from the publisher's extensive library of color photographs. Then came the task of photographing the plants not represented in the publisher's library. Several horticultural photographers were assigned specific subjects to photograph. After first locating the subject, a constant vigil was maintained in order to catch the star at its photogenic best. As illustrations were selected for each of the eight classifications, they were given to horticultural writers for compiling accurate descriptions of each subject. The results of this judicious culling and selecting are represented in this volume of 438 illustrations.

Every illustration is reproduced by lithography from a color transparency. Four lithographic halftone negatives are made from the original transparency, representing the four colors of ink used in printing; namely, yellow, blue, red and black. Each of these four pieces of film are hand corrected before making proofing plates to insure faithful color reproduction. Each page is then color proofed in the exact manner of the final printing. These proofs are carefully checked for accuracy of color and where necessary, further color corrections are made. Several cycles of color correcting and proofing have been necessary of a few pages to achieve color fidelity demanded of this volume.

The objective in publishing "GARDEN PLANTS IN COLOR" is to provide a practical tool for the horticulturist.

The home gardener can use it to advantage in landscaping the home. Nurserymen, landscape architects, and gardeners will recognize the dual intent of this volume as sales manual and planting guide. Through its use customers can more readily visualize a specific plant in full foliage, blooming, or fruiting as it will grow in the garden. Sales personnel with the use of this book, can give a convincing sales presentation based upon accurate information concerning the plants being sold and provide comprehensive answers to questions about growing habits, ultimate size and degree of hardiness of a particular variety.

Each of the eight classifications of plants is prefaced with an enlightening introduction that will enable the reader to more fully understand and appreciate its value and importance in landscaping. Each of these introductions is written by horticulturists with many years of experience in propagating, hybridizing, and promoting the cultivation of plants illustrated in their assigned classification.

Illustrations of varieties within each section appear in alphabetical order by botanical name, except for the last two pages in the Rhododendron section which are supplements. **Bold face type** of the captions indicates the approved scientific name. SMALL CAPITALS indicate approved horticultural variety and common names. *Italic type* denotes synonyms. Beneath each illustration appears the publisher's library index number for that subject. This number identifies the specific illustration and distinguishes it from other illustrations of the same variety.

The zone map of cold hardiness has been compiled from data secured by the United States Department of Agriculture in cooperation with the American Horticultural Council. This map affords a visual means of educating customers and students of horticulture in the importance of proper plant selection for a given temperature zone.

The final pages contain a complete listing of plants illustrated in this volume. This is a cross index listing the botanical names (bold face type), common names (small capitals) and synonyms (italic type) in alphabetical order. Opposite each plant named is the number of the section in which the plant is illustrated and the page on which it appears. This index provides a quick, convenient means of locating the section and page on which a plant is illustrated.

The contents of "GARDEN PLANTS IN COLOR" represents the ideas, suggestions, criticisms and contributions of literally hundreds of horticulturists from all sections of the country. The publisher is indeed grateful for each and every contribution of time and energy so generously given by friends and associates.

Our Editor

HENRY T. SKINNER has had a long-time interest in plants. Born in England, he received early training at the Wisley Gardens of the Royal Horticultural Society. Coming to this country in 1929, he studied at the Arnold Arboretum under the directorship of "Chinese" Wilson before teaching horticulture for nine years at Cornell University. He was Curator of the Morris Arboretum in Philadelphia until his appointment as director of the U. S. National Arboretum in Washington, D. C., in 1952. Dr. Skinner holds degrees in horticulture and botany from Cornell University and the University of Pennsylvania, and is the recipient of the Jackson Dawson Medal of the Massachusetts Horticultural Society. He is known for his writing on horticultural topics, and for his participation in many horticultural organizations. A past president of the American Association of Botanic Gardens and Arboretums, he is currently an officer of the American Horticultural Society and the American Horticultural Council.

Contributors

BRIAN O. MULLIGAN also began his horticultural training at the Gardens of the Royal Horticultural Society in England. After experience in several English nurseries and spending four years in research work at Long Ashton Research Station, University of Bristol, he returned to Wisley in 1935 as assistant to the Director. Following service in the R.A.F., he became Horticultural Advisor to the Air Ministry from 1942 to 1946 when he was released to return to Wisley. He is now Director of the University of Washington Arboretum at Seattle, past president of the American Association of Botanic Gardens and Arboretums, and vice president of the American Rock Garden Society. He has recently compiled a *Check List of Maples Cultivated in the United States and Canada* for publication by the American Association of Botanic Gardens and Arboretums.

WILLIAM FLEMER, III was born at Princeton, New Jersey, and is a graduate of Yale University where he received a B.A. Degree in Botany and his Masters Degree in Plant Physiology. After serving three years in the United States Army, he joined the Princeton Nurseries in 1947 where he is now vice president and general manager. Mr. Flemer is past president of the American Nurserymen's Protective Association and a member of the Board of Governors of the American Association of Nurserymen. He has contributed articles for *Plants and Gardens* Magazine and Bulletin of the Torrey Botanical Club, and is a frequent lecturer to trade, municipal, and garden organizations.

R. L. HUDSON began horticultural training in 1931 at the Golden Gate Park where he became propagator. In 1941 he landscaped the San Francisco Zoological Gardens. He was appointed Supervisor of Maintenance of the San Francisco Park Department in 1945 and now continues in that capacity. Mr. Hudson is a founding member of the California Horticultural Society, corresponding member of the American Rhododendron Society, member of California Chapter of American Institute of Park Executives, and frequent lecturer to garden clubs. He is author of *Sunset Pruning Handbook* and a frequent contributor to the Journal of the California Horticultural Society and the Quarterly Bulletins of the American Rhododendron Society.

P. H. BRYDON received his early horticultural training in Edinburgh, Scotland and the University of California in Berkeley. He was lecturer in Plant Propagation at the University of California and a frequent lecturer to garden groups and horticultural associations. He has written numerous articles for bulletins of the American Rhododendron Society, American Horticultural Society, California Horticultural Society and various garden magazines. He now owns and operates Brydon's Nursery in Salem, Oregon, and specializes in Rhododendrons and Azaleas.

VERNON R. JAMES attended the University of Colorado. At the termination of World War II he entered the nursery business at Los Gatos, California, and began intensive study and research in camellia propagation and hybridization. He now owns and operates a nursery with his son at Aptos, California, where he is continuing important work in the propagation of camellias. He has contributed articles to newspaper garden sections and Camellia Society bulletins and publications. He is a charter member of All America Camellia Selections, Inc., and an accredited judge of the American Camellia Society.

L. L. KUMLIEN has had many years of practical experience in the nursery business. He was associated with the D. Hill Nurseries at Dundee, Illinois, for over 30 years and has been co-owner with his son of a nursery in Janesville, Wisconsin, for the past 12 years. Mr. Kumlien has made an intensive study of coniferous evergreens and is the author of *The Friendly Evergreens*, a nontechnical book, published in 1946. He also authored *Hill's Book of Evergreens* published in 1936.

JACK M. STORY attended the University of California at Berkeley. He has been employed by Armstrong Nurseries in Ontario, California, since 1934 excluding three years' service in the Army Air Corps during World War II. Currently he is director of his company's advertising and publicity program. He is a frequent lecturer before garden clubs and a regular contributor of articles on gardening to home magazine sections of California newspapers. Mr. Story has served three years on the Publicity Committee of the California Association of Nurserymen and is now a member of the State Board of Directors of that organization.

Garden Plants in Color

Contents

GARDEN PLANTS IN COLOR

Introduction

TREES AND SHRUBS provide the structural material of the landscape. They are the relatively permanent elements and because of this permanence they should be chosen with care and so used as to provide both pleasing and lasting contributions to the landscape pattern. For any plant, however, such attributes as quality, habit, appearance and effectiveness are difficult to describe. The gardener or home owner is more often confused rather than helped by written descriptions, the nurseryman finds difficulty in selling his young stock in terms of mature appearance, and the teacher finds similar problems in the absence of living specimens or suitable exhibit material.

Effective illustration is the best substitute for the plant itself. Customers have learned this through the use of well-illustrated catalogs, nurserymen through the success of such catalogs, and teachers through their similar use of text figures, color slides, and so on. Color photography provides the modern, most generally accurate and most effective medium of illustration. But color reproduction is expensive and because of this, with few exceptions, it has been used in horticultural texts on a decorative, rather than systematic, basis. This volume is among the first of its kind to provide natural color illustrations of a wide selection of woody plants with each illustration arranged and indexed for easy finding. Conceived as a source listing of available illustrations of trees and shrubs, it has evolved by stages to its present form as an intended reference manual for gardeners, students and plant purchasers, and as an adaptable sales manual for the nursery industry.

Within the eight major groups of trees, shrubs, vines and ground covers chosen for coverage in this book, the task of individual plant selection has posed a variety of problems. Subject to the unavoidable limitations of space and cost, it is obvious that not all trees and shrubs — not even all the best trees and shrubs — could be included. But since needs of the average gardener and the average nurseryman were of primary consideration, selection has been necessarily based upon the twin criteria of quality and general commercial availability. Admittedly this has resulted in the exclusion of some well-known and many lesser-known but excellent plants.

The selective procedure has consisted of the submission of tentative plant lists for their checking and criticism by various authorities in different sections of the country. So far as was then possible, color photographs were selected of the chosen specimens. Such photographs have been accumulated over many years and they have inevitably varied in quality. A recommended plant, intended for inclusion, is sometimes lacking for want of a better or more typical illustration, in spite of the fact that many new pictures have been taken especially for use here during the past two years.

An alphabetic arrangement by plant names has proved to be the most usable system in a reference designed for national coverage. While there would be convenience in grouping on regional or climatic bases, it is evident that many plants are susceptible to cultivation over such wide areas that the duplications of such regional treatments would be unduly complicated. It is believed that the climatic data provided will give both a clear and reliable picture of regional climatic adaptability.

Illustrations have been selected to portray as accurately as possible the principal or most distinctive characteristics of each subject, whether such characteristics be habit and appearance at maturity, flower form and color, quality of foliage, or distinctive fruit. More than one illustration per plant has sometimes been necessary to achieve this objective. Botanical names conform to modern accepted usage and include synonyms when older names may still be the most familiar. The decapitalization of all specific names and use of single "i" terminals (e.g. *Pinus griffithi* rather than *Pinus Griffithii*) also follows the pattern of current non-technical practice. The treatment of varietal names requires a word or two of explanation.

The new (1958) International Code of Horticultural Nomenclature prescribes the exclusive use of English (non-Latin) names for horticultural varieties or "cultivars," such names being differentiated from the botanical species name by use of a capitalized first letter and a different type form in printing, or by enclosure of the name in single quotes. A new yew to be named in honor of Mr. Jones would thus become *Taxus cuspidata* 'Jones' or 'Jones Upright' rather than the now illegitimate *Taxus cuspidata Jonesii* or *jonesi*. But a latinized varietal name given before 1959 will remain in good standing and may be optionally written in its original form as *Taxus baccata washingtoni*, or, in clearer expression of its horticultural origin, as

Taxus baccata 'Washingtoni.' The text following is inconsistent to the extent that neither of these optional systems is used exclusively. The single-quote designation (*Thuja occidentalis* 'Woodwardi') has been used where it has seemed to be reasonably logical and convenient while traditional name forms as *Juniperus virginiana tripartita* have been retained when the optional transition to 'Tripartita' seems somewhat strained. It is hoped that mixed usage of this sort may encourage familiarity with a recommended system for designating varietal names without causing unnecessary confusion.

The caption descriptions are intended as brief guides to the principal characteristics of a tree or shrub, as well as to the ordinary or special growing conditions such a plant may require. The expression of hardiness in terms of temperature tolerance rather than on a zone basis eliminates the necessity for constant reference to a hardiness map while permitting interpretation in terms of such a map if the need arises. A word of caution is, nevertheless, in order. Due possibly to a longer growing season, temperature tolerances may be several degrees higher on the west coast than for the same plant grown in the central or eastern states. This may not be of great import, but is sometimes confusing to the person whose plant may survive lower temperatures than it "officially" should.

"GARDEN PLANTS IN COLOR" is available in two types of bindings. The library edition is contained in a hand bound cover with pages sewn in. The loose leaf binder is designed for the ready removal or substitution of individual pages by professional horticulturists. The contents and cover material of the two editions are identical.

SEE FULL SIZE MAP
ON INSIDE SPREAD

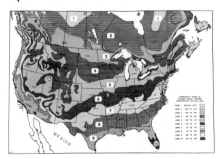

Zone Map of Cold Hardiness

The ten zones of this hardiness map represent geographic areas differentiated on a basis of average minimum winter temperature. By comparing hardiness figures for the plants of this book with the zone temperatures of this map, the northern or coldest limits of likely performance can be readily determined. Each plant may be expected to be winter hardy from the selected zone into warmer areas but not in those which are more northerly and colder.

Cold hardiness is one of many factors influencing the geographical survival and adaptability of plants. But information concerning it is helpful because it is also one of the most important of these climatic factors.

This map prepared from data furnished by the United States Department of Agriculture.

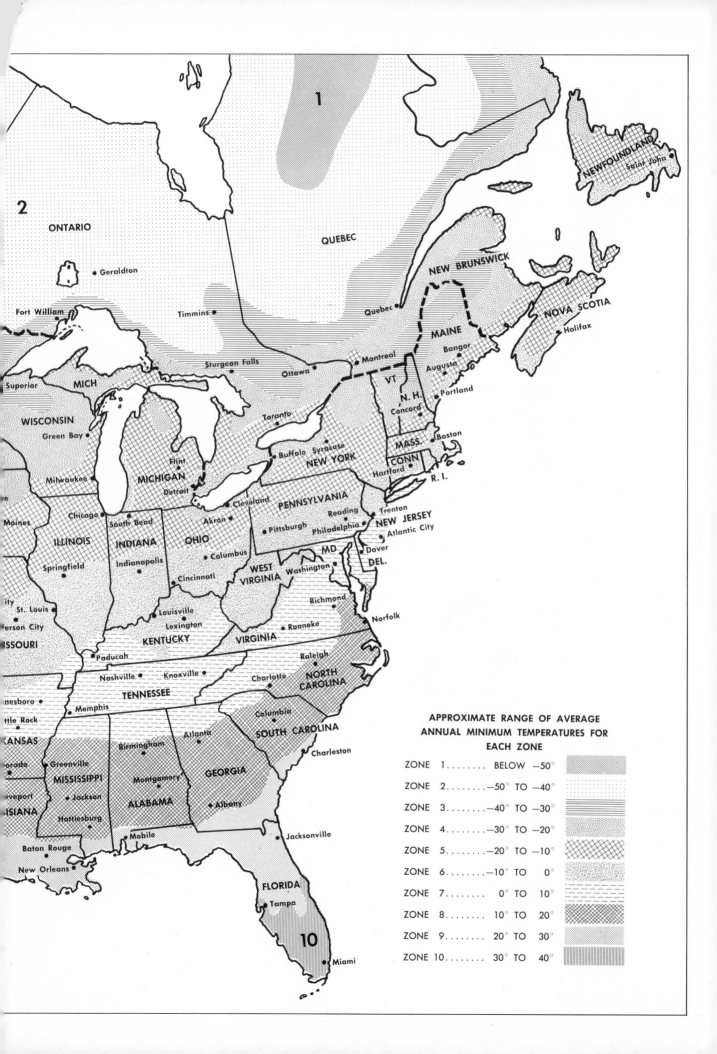

1

2

ONTARIO

• Geraldton

Fort William •

Timmins •

QUEBEC

Sturgeon Falls •

Superior

WISCONSIN

MICH

Green Bay •

Milwaukee •

Flint •

MICHIGAN

Detroit •

Chicago •

South Bend •

Akron •

Cleveland •

Moines

ILLINOIS

INDIANA

OHIO

Columbus •

Springfield •

Indianapolis •

Cincinnati •

ity

St. Louis •

Louisville •

erson City

Lexington •

SSOURI

KENTUCKY

• Paducah

Nashville •

Knoxville •

nesboro •

ttle Rock •

Memphis •

ANSAS

orado •

Greenville •

MISSISSIPPI

Birmingham •

Montgomery •

eveport

• Jackson

ALABAMA

ISIANA

Hattiesburg •

Mobile •

Baton Rouge •

New Orleans •

NEWFOUNDLAND

Saint John •

NEW BRUNSWICK

NOVA SCOTIA

Quebec •

Halifax •

MAINE

Bangor •

Montreal •

Augusta •

VT

Portland •

Ottawa •

N.H.

Concord •

Toronto •

MASS

• Boston

Buffalo • Syracuse •

CONN

NEW YORK

Hartford •

R. I.

PENNSYLVANIA

Reading •

Trenton •

Pittsburgh •

Philadelphia •

NEW JERSEY

Washington •

MD

Dover •

• Atlantic City

WEST VIRGINIA

DEL.

Richmond •

Norfolk •

Roanoke •

VIRGINIA

Raleigh •

Charlotte •

NORTH CAROLINA

Columbia •

Atlanta •

SOUTH CAROLINA

Charleston •

GEORGIA

• Albany

Jacksonville •

FLORIDA

Tampa •

10

• Miami

APPROXIMATE RANGE OF AVERAGE
ANNUAL MINIMUM TEMPERATURES FOR
EACH ZONE

ZONE 1........ BELOW −50°

ZONE 2........−50° TO −40°

ZONE 3........−40° TO −30°

ZONE 4........−30° TO −20°

ZONE 5........−20° TO −10°

ZONE 6........−10° TO   0°

ZONE 7........   0° TO 10°

ZONE 8........ 10° TO 20°

ZONE 9........ 20° TO 30°

ZONE 10........ 30° TO 40°

Trees—Shade and Flowering

Section 10

TREES—SHADE AND FLOWERING

Introduction

MOST TREES are easily recognized as such and generally well separated from other plants by their height and size, by possessing a single stem or trunk, and an extensive system of strong branches bearing the leaves, flowers, and later in the year fruits.

Sometimes, however, it is difficult in practice to distinguish large, single-stemmed shrubs, such as some rhododendrons, camellias, junipers and *Ligustrum* species, from small multi-stemmed trees, for example *Arbutus unedo*, the strawberry tree, *Magnolia virginiana*, or the *Franklinia*. In such cases they can be included in either group, depending chiefly upon their size and form.

We are here concerned with definite and distinct trees, those which we expect to grow from perhaps 15 to 20 feet in the smaller types to 50 or 60 feet in the larger species, to give us shade in summer, flowers in spring or later, and perhaps attractive fruits or fall leaf color in due season.

There are not too many trees which can provide even three of these desirable four characters in one individual, but it is important to remember them and try to plant one which will be beautiful for more than a single short period of the year. Crabapples, some plums, cherries, service berries and oaks, larches, hawthorns, mountain ashes, several *Stuartia* species, the Norway maple, Katsura tree *(Cercidiphyllum)* and the sourwood *(Oxydendrum)* are examples.

Among trees there is a vast variety in size and form of species, in color, shape and size of foliage, flowers and fruits, and in many other features, so that we can have every extreme, if we wish, from giant sequoia trees or redwoods down to the pigmy specimens exemplified by some of the naturally dwarf conifers.

Types of Trees

(a) EVERGREEN TREES

These must be again subdivided into (1) the conifers, or cone-bearing trees, which are dealt with in another section of this work, and (2) broad-leaved evergreen trees, very different in appearance, in garden values, and often in hardiness.

Some of the latter are extremely valuable and much used, especially in warm or temperate climates: *Magnolia grandiflora*, various hollies *(Ilex)*, the Portugal laurel *(Prunus lusitanica)*, the bay *(Laurus nobilis)*, the strawberry tree *(Arbutus unedo)* and madrono or madrona *(A. menziesi)* readily come to mind.

Others likewise planted in some areas include the evergreen oaks, both native American as well as European or Asiatic, the California laurel or Oregon myrtle *(Umbellularia californica)*, *Ligustrum lucidum*, *Pittosporum* and *Eucalyptus* species, with a variety of others. In colder climates, where the thermometer reaches zero in most winters, few if any of these can be successfully grown. The Portugal laurel, madrono, American holly *(Ilex opaca)*, *Ilex pedunculosa* and *I. integra* from Ja-

Trees—Shade and Flowering (Continued)

pan, and the California laurel are among the hardiest species.

Where any of these can be utilized they are of considerable landscape value—some for their flowers or fruits as well as for evergreen effect.

(b) DECIDUOUS TREES

Here we have a much wider selection to choose from, to suit all kinds of climates, tastes and wishes, although still by no means as large as it could be, or will be in another quarter century when the wealth of available material in our arboreta and botanic gardens has been more fully evaluated and drawn upon.

Some of the best now available are to be found among the following:

1. Flowering trees

Catalpas, cherries, crabapples, dogwoods, empress tree *(Paulownia)*, golden rain tree *(Koelreuteria)*, hawthorns, horse chestnuts, laburnums, locusts, magnolias, pagoda tree *(Sophora japonica)*, plums, redbuds, silk tree *(Albizzia)*, silverbell *(Halesia)*, *Stuartia* species, and *Styrax japonica*.

2. Trees for ornamental fruits

Arbutus species, crabapples, *Cotoneaster frigida*, *Euonymus bungeana*, *E. europaea* and other species, hawthorns, hollies, mountain ashes, *Photinia* species, sea buckthorn *(Hippophae)*, tree-of-heaven *(Ailanthus)*.

3. Trees for fall color

Maples, dogwoods, Katsura tree, *Franklinia*, sourwood *(Oxydendrum)*, tupelo or black gum *(Nyssa sylvatica)*,

various oaks, especially red, scarlet, black, pin and shingle oaks, Sargent's cherry, shadbushes or service berries *(Amelanchier* species), yellow and other birches, *Ginkgo, Sorbus alnifolia, Stuartia* species, sweet gum *(Liquidambar)*, sassafras, and tulip tree *(Liriodendron)*.

Trees in the Landscape

It is hardly possible to omit one or more trees in any planting plan, except in the smallest areas, and even there it should be possible to place one of appropriate size and in scale.

Before any other planting is done on a new site the position of all required trees should be decided, the sites marked and the kinds to be used determined. It is important to place them where they will have ample room to grow to maturity without interfering with buildings, roads, overhead power or telephone lines or any other more or less permanent structures.

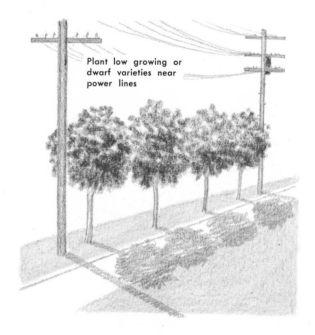

Plant low growing or dwarf varieties near power lines

Trees—Shade and Flowering *(Continued)*

The effect they will have on the landscape should be judged both from the approaches to the area and buildings, and from the latter themselves. The shape of the trees should harmonize with any neighboring structures, avoiding, for example, upright types in conjunction with low one-story buildings.

Too tall

Obstructs driveway

Blocks view

WRONG

Low growing trees in harmony with single story dwellings

CORRECT

Avenues should generally consist of one kind of tree; if the approach is wide, and a double avenue is possible, then a tall species may be in the rear, a shorter in front, to be effective at different seasons; e.g. pines in the background, cherries or crabapples in front.

Groups of 3 to 5 trees are usually preferable to single specimens, unless the site is small and a single oak or other large tree is desired. They should be planted far enough apart to meet when mature, but not so close as to crowd or spoil one another.

Single specimens should be most carefully chosen, with due regard to the site conditions and the purposes for which they are needed.

The winter effect of planting a group of white-stemmed birches in front of pines or other evergreens is well known; the value of purple, grey or golden-leaved trees, and of mass planting for particular effects or contrasts at one or more seasons should not be forgotten.

There is infinite scope for pleasing combinations of form and color, in both foliage and flowers.

Cultivation

The three most important factors in ensuring successful tree plantings are:

1. The tree itself, including an adequate root system which should be sufficiently extensive to provide a large enough ball of roots to support the head of branches. If the roots have been chopped off short then the top must be pruned back hard to balance their loss. Such root treatment, however, is unnecessary and thoroughly bad practice.

Trees—Shade and Flowering (Continued)

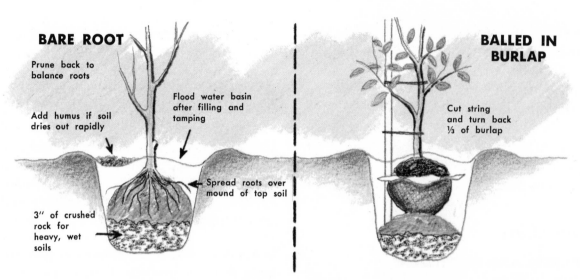

BARE ROOT

Prune back to balance roots

Flood water basin after filling and tamping

Add humus if soil dries out rapidly

Spread roots over mound of top soil

3″ of crushed rock for heavy, wet soils

BALLED IN BURLAP

Cut string and turn back ⅓ of burlap

2. The preparation of the site, which will depend upon the soil conditions encountered. If heavy, and probably wet in certain seasons, then either proper drainage for excess water must be provided, or a type of tree planted which will tolerate such conditions; as examples, alders, some species of ash, birches, swamp cypress, Japanese larch, and willows.

If the soil is light and dries out in summer, materials such as compost, leaf mold, humus from woods, or old farm or stable manure, should be added to give the young tree a good start; a thick mulch of some suitable material should also cover more than the planting area after completion of the job. The chosen species should be known to tolerate, if not like, such soils; e.g., birches, box elders, junipers, locusts, pines.

In each case the soil should be excavated to form a hole both wider and deeper than the size of the root ball, and loosened beneath to permit the young roots to penetrate downwards for moisture.

3. The actual planting. Natural soil and any added materials should be well mixed.

A stake should be driven in firmly on the windward side of the tree *before* filling takes place, and the tree tied after the soil is all firmly trodden in, either with several turns of a thick weatherproof cord, or preferably with a strip of old tire rubber nailed to the post, or a length of old rubber hose with a heavy wire through it twisted around tree and post. More than one such tie will be needed on trees seven feet high or taller. A guard formed of a circle of chicken wire at least 36 inches high may be necessary if dogs or cats are likely to be a nuisance.

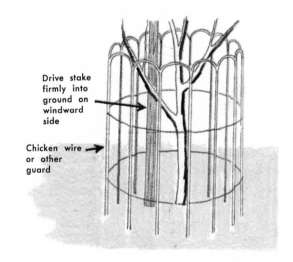

Drive stake firmly into ground on windward side

Chicken wire or other guard

Trees—Shade and Flowering (Continued)

The time of planting will largely depend upon local climatic conditions; but where the weather permits, fall or early winter planting, when the young trees can make some new growth at once and then become dormant, is preferable to waiting until March or April. Trees planted in spring always require more care to establish than those set out four months earlier.

Later Care

PRUNING AND FERTILIZING

The first year or two are naturally the most important in starting a tree in its permanent place, and probably the supply of water during the first summer is the chief factor in determining not only whether it lives or dies, but how far it extends its root system and becomes established — hence the prime importance of preparing the site deeply.

If watering is necessary, then it should be done regularly, perhaps once a week during the hottest periods, and thoroughly, so that the whole root area is soaked, not merely the surface. To aid this it is well when planting, especially in spring, to leave a slight basin of soil around the stem in which water can collect and not run off.

As a general rule young trees should be pruned quite hard, up to one-half of their young wood being removed, in order to form a strong, well-branched head. In later years thinning out and removal of low, crossing, or other undesirable branches is usually all that is necessary. Much, if not all, of such work can be done in late summer or early fall.

If a tree occupies a site of limited space, then pruning should be done to an upward pointing bud, to restrict its spread as much as possible; or pyramidal or columnar forms of trees can be used, of which examples are to be found in red and sugar maples, European hornbeam and mountain ash, Japanese cherry ('Amanogawa'), ginkgo, European and American elms ('Augustine' and 'Moline') and other kinds.

Applying fertilizer to trees is a much more difficult problem than giving it to shrubs or vegetable crops, especially if the trees are surrounded by a thick grass sod or by paving.

In the latter case most of the fertilizer will have to be given in the form of liquid applications to the foliage during the summer (June-July). Large trees growing in grass will require the method of boring holes with an auger or crowbar in circles around the outer two-thirds of the area covered by the branches, and slightly beyond. These holes should be 15-18 inches deep, 2 feet apart, and slope slightly inward towards the base. About 3 lbs. of a complete fertilizer (10-8-6 or 10-6-4 formula) per inch of trunk diameter, for larger trees, will be needed for distribution in the holes, which are then filled in again with soil. Times of application: either in fall (October) for early spring use by the tree, or in February-April for summer use, but the earlier the better. For small trees, if old stable or barnyard manure is available and can be used, a mulch over the entire root system will work wonders in one season. If commercial fertilizers only are possible, then use half the above rate.

2358

Acacia baileyana
Cootamundra-Wattle

Large, spreading, fast growing tree to 30 feet, with spreading habit and deeply cut silvery-green foliage. Completely covered for many weeks in late winter and early spring with sprays of fragrant yellow flowers. Prefers semi-drought conditions and is hardy to about 10 degrees above zero.

Acer negundo variegatum
Variegated Box Elder

A medium sized deciduous tree, which grows rapidly to 30 feet or so; rather slender with a rounded crown of light green leaves, margined silver. Does well in nearly all soils and climates and is hardy below zero, but is brittle and considered relatively short-lived.

LS475

Acer palmatum ornatum
LACELEAF JAPANESE MAPLE

A picturesque small deciduous tree, irregular in shape and airy with its fern-like, deeply cut foliage. New leaves are red turning to soft green in summer and changing back to scarlet in the fall. Grows slowly to about 12 feet, preferably in filtered sunlight. Excellent in containers. Good soil, plenty of moisture. Hardy to zero.

Acer palmatum atropurpureum
PURPLE-LEAVED JAPANESE MAPLE

A most attractive small tree of bushy habit, attaining 15 to 20 feet in height and spread; foliage a deep maroon red all summer. Enjoys a neutral or slightly acid soil, partial shade, and an annual mulch of leaves or compost. Makes an excellent lawn specimen. Hardy to below zero, especially in well-drained sites.

LS651

1704

Acer platanoides 'Crimson King'
Norway Maple Crimson King
(Plant Patent No. 735)

Fast-growing, upright, deciduous shade tree to 45 feet, with a spread of 25 feet. The broad foliage is attractively colored bright red when new and reddish-purple throughout the spring and summer months. Will tolerate wide variations in soil and climate but not at its best in hot arid sections and, though suffering from extremes of freezing weather, will withstand steady winter temperatures below zero.

Acer platanoides
Norway Maple

Rapid growth to height of 50 to 60 feet with spread of 40 to 50 feet. Forms a wide-spreading, dense, rounded crown with large bright green leaves turning to bright yellow before dropping in the fall. Grows readily under adverse climatic and soil conditions. Is hardy to about 10 degrees below zero.

LS493

Acer platanoides 'Schwedleri'
SCHWEDLER NORWAY MAPLE

Smaller tree than *Acer platanoides*. Foliage is red in spring turning to green in summer then changing to brilliant hues of gold before dropping in the fall. Resists cold temperatures to below zero. Should be given protection from direct sun.

LS437

LS652

Acer pseudo-platanus 'Albovariegatum'
VARIEGATED SYCAMORE MAPLE

Large, vigorous, spreading deciduous tree to 50 feet or more with spread from 30 to 50 feet. Big 5-lobed leaves to 7 inches across are light green, blotched and spotted with white. Thrives even in exposed areas with good soil and ample moisture, but not well suited to hot arid sections. Hardy below zero.

Acer saccharinum
SILVER MAPLE

Large, very fast-growing deciduous shade tree from 30 to 60 feet tall, with 30 to 60 feet spread. Typical maple leaves are light green above and silvery beneath. There is a good show of yellow autumn color in colder areas. Probably the best maple for hot arid regions, but likes plenty of water. Hardy below zero.

LS408

LS459

Alnus rhombifolia
SIERRA ALDER

The common alder of the Coast Range Mountains from British Columbia to southern California. A fast-growing deciduous erect tree from 40 to 100 feet high with spread of 20 to 40 feet. Dense attractive foliage. Likes constant moisture. Hardy.

2384

Albizzia julibrissin
SILKTREE ALBIZZIA

Fast-growing deciduous shade tree — irregular, spreading, and picturesque, from 25 to 40 feet in height, 15 to 40 feet spread. Has dark green fern-like foliage and in mid-summer is covered with fluffy pink flowers. Tolerant of most soils, dry or wet, and hardy to about zero.

LS168

Aesculus carnea
RED HORSE-CHESTNUT

A round-headed deciduous tree growing moderately fast to about 40 feet, with the same spread. Thickly covered with dark green leaves, it provides fine deep summer shade. In April and May the tree is a mass of bloom — soft pink to red or scarlet. Reasonably trouble-free and recommended in some areas as a street tree. Drought resistant, but prefers rich loamy soil. Hardy zero or below.

2161

Bauhinia variegata 'Candida'
WHITE ORCHID TREE

A color variation quite common in Bauhinias is this white-flowered form. It is just like *Bauhinia variegata* in all particulars, except that the flowers are creamy-white.

1132

Betula pendula
EUROPEAN WHITE BIRCH
Syn. *B. alba*

Tall, slender deciduous tree with a straight trunk and semi-weeping branches, spreading from 8 to 15 feet. The white bark, dancing foliage and a lacy look make it a very popular ornamental. Grows from 25 to 40 feet, likes moisture, and is hardy.

LS653

Bauhinia variegata
PURPLE ORCHID TREE

Small, spreading, deciduous umbrella-like tree which grows rather slowly, from 15 to 20 feet, with a spread of 15 to 20 feet. The large two-lobed leaves of soft green give way for a while in the spring to a profusion of big orchid-like flowers of deep pinkish-lavender, marked with purple and yellow. Hardy only to about 22 degrees.

Chionanthus virginicus
WHITE FRINGE TREE

Graceful small tree with large oval leaves, slow growing to about 20 by 20 feet, rather open and airy in habit. In May and June lacy 6-inch panicles of little white flowers hang from each branch. Adaptable to most soils and climates and hardy below zero degrees.

LS654

Ceratonia siliqua
CAROB, ST. JOHN'S BREAD

A symmetrical, dense, round-headed evergreen tree which grows moderately fast to about 40 feet and spreads from 20 to 30 feet. Widely used for parkways or as a home shade tree. Will stand heat and considerable drought. Hardy to about 12 degrees above zero.

2292

Cercis canadensis
EASTERN REDBUD

A showy small rounded deciduous tree growing about 15 feet tall and as much in spread. Before the leaves appear in early spring, the branches are crowded with clusters of rose-colored sweet-pea-like blooms. Easily grown almost anywhere and hardy below zero degrees.

LS655

LS328

Cinnamomum camphora
CAMPHOR-TREE

Grows rather slowly to about 50 feet, sometimes attaining a spread of 80 feet or more. It is a clean, hardy, deep-rooted tree with regular form and handsome evergreen foliage. Fine for parkways or as an evergreen shade tree. Hardy to about 10 degrees above zero.

LS656

Cornus florida
FLOWERING DOGWOOD

Good looking little tree, deciduous and notable for its great spring show of creamy-white flower bracts. Grows 20 to 25 feet in height and 12 to 15 feet in spread. Prefers semi-shade, acid soil and plenty of moisture. Hardy below zero degrees.

Cornus florida rubra
PINK FLOWERING DOGWOOD

Small deciduous tree, sometimes to 20 feet, with a spread of 12 to 15 feet. Covered with showy 4-inch pink flowers before the foliage appears in spring. Best in cooler areas, but hardy anywhere.

LS657

Crataegus crus-galli
COCKSPUR HAWTHORN

A small- to medium-sized tree, with a very dense, more or less horizontal branch system spreading from 15 to 30 feet and numerous long stout thorns, providing the common name. Flowers white, in clusters, late May to early June; fruit less than ½ inch wide, glossy, dark red, hanging until January. Hardy to 15-20 degrees below zero.

▽ Crataegus oxyacantha 'Pauli'
PAUL'S DOUBLE SCARLET HAWTHORN

Colorful small tree reaching 25 to 30 feet in height, spreading 15 to 20 feet. In May covered with innumerable double red flowers. Frequently used with success for street plantings, bearing no fruits. Hardy to about 15 degrees below zero.

LS658

2397

Elaeagnus angustifolia
RUSSIAN OLIVE

Small, spiny, deciduous tree, 15 to 20 feet high with a spread of 10 to 15 feet. Grows rapidly in picturesque, irregular shape. Has handsome silvery-gray foliage and yellow berries with silvery scales in late summer. Hardy everywhere.

LS442

2417

Ficus retusa
INDIAN LAUREL FIG

Most widely planted of the rubber trees. A handsome evergreen tree which grows rapidly to about 40 feet with a spread to 20 feet, and is covered densely with dark green 2 to 4-inch leaves. Grows well where roots are restricted and may be trained or pruned to any desired height. Successful where temperatures do not fall below 20 degrees above zero.

LS659

Eriobotrya japonica
LOQUAT

Very ornamental, small evergreen tree with large tropical-looking leaves. Grows 15 to 20 feet tall, and as much across. Loaded in early spring with tangy edible yellow fruits. Hardy for a sub-tropical, withstanding temperatures of 10 degrees above zero.

Fraxinus pennsylvanica lanceolata
GREEN ASH

Moderately fast-growing shade tree, 30 to 50 feet high, spreading 20 to 30 feet. Has a compact oval crown and is densely clothed with large bright green foliage. Hardy below zero, but apt to suffer from leaf burn in hot arid situations.

LS443

LS369

Fraxinus velutina glabra
MODESTO ASH

Deciduous shade tree with a symmetrical crown of smooth, shiny, green leaves. Grows fairly fast to 30 or 40 feet, spreading 15 to 20 feet. Leafs out early in spring and holds foliage well into winter. Tolerates considerable alkalinity, much heat and drought, and is hardy to zero degrees.

LS650

Gleditsia triacanthos inermis
MORAINE® LOCUST (Plant Patent 836)

Fast-growing deciduous tree, 40 to 60 feet tall, and as much across. Fern-like foliage gives airy summer shade and provides considerable fall color. This preferred form does not have the objectionable thorns nor pods of the common honey locust. Will grow in almost any soil, or under any conditions, and is hardy well below zero.

LS333

Ginkgo biloba
MAIDENHAIR TREE

Rather slow-growing deciduous tree, which is generally pyramidal, but open and airy in habit, and which ultimately may grow to 60 feet or more, spreading 30 to 60 feet. The leathery fan-shaped leaves are light green in spring and summer, turn to golden yellow in fall, then drop off slowly. Likes good deep soil, but will stand considerable heat and drought and is hardy. Very tolerant of city conditions and one of the few trees useful for fall color in the southwest.

LS660

LS661

LS647

Heteromeles arbutifolia Syn. *Photinia arbutifolia*
◁ CALIFORNIA HOLLY (TOYON)

Large shrub or irregular, many-branched, small tree to 15 or 20 feet. Clothed throughout the year with thick glossy leaves. In late fall has big clusters of showy bright red berries, fine for Christmas decoration. Needs good drainage and full sun. Hardy to about 15 degrees above zero.

Harpephyllum caffrum
KAFIR PLUM

Fast-growing to height of 30 feet forming a round head with a spread of about 20 feet. New foliage is bright red, changing to dark green when mature. Bears edible dark red fruit which ripens in summer. At its best in mild coastal climates. Hardy to about 30 degrees above zero. Prefers light, moist, well-drained soil.

Ilex aquifolium
ENGLISH HOLLY

One of the handsomest evergreen medium sized trees, to about 40 feet tall and up to 20 feet spread, where it can be successfully grown. Foliage glossy, shiny, dark green, or variegated in some forms; flowers inconspicuous, May-June, male and female flowers borne on separate trees. Fruits bright shining red, November-March; also a yellow form. Likes shade from hot sun, a rather light and well-drained soil, but with ample humus. Hardy to about zero.

2164

Jacaranda acutifolia
JACARANDA

Picturesque evergreen tree, usually rather open with a spreading head. Ultimately 30 to 40 feet tall, with spread to 30 feet or so. Finely cut fern-like foliage gives a lacy look and the tree is spectacular in June when covered with clouds of blue blooms. Prefers well-drained soil, some protection from strong winds, and is hardy to about 22 degrees above zero.

LS182

Juglans regia
ENGLISH WALNUT

Several varieties are the standard walnuts of commerce. Fast-growing, the big, rounded, deciduous trees often reach 60 to 70 feet, with a spread of 40 to 70 feet. Makes a fine, fruiting shade tree where space is available and temperatures are moderate. Needs good, deep soil. Hardy to about 5 degrees below zero.

LS500

Koelreuteria paniculata
PANICLED GOLDEN RAIN TREE

A rather slow-growing deciduous tree from 20 to 30 feet tall, with a spread of 15 to 20 feet. Has handsome foliage and is loaded in June and July with showy foot-long panicles of bright yellow flowers. Tolerates poor soil, alkalinity, considerable heat. Hardy below zero.

LS544

Laburnum watereri   Syn. *L. Vossi*
LONGCLUSTER GOLDEN CHAIN TREE

Small tree growing fairly fast under good conditions to 20 feet or more, with a spread of about 15 feet. The bark is light green and the compound leaves are gray-green. In spring displays wisteria-like flower panicles of bright yellow, up to 1½ feet long. Best in partial shade in warmer areas and likes lime. Needs cold winters for best flowers. Hardy below zero.

LS662

Liquidambar styraciflua
AMERICAN SWEETGUM

Tall pyramidal tree with handsome maple-like leaves. Grows moderately from 40 to 60 feet, with a spread of 15 to 30 feet. This tree is a very desirable ornamental — one of the few which will show autumn reds and golds in warm-wintered sections. Thrives almost anywhere and is hardy below zero.

1770

LS646

LS407

Malus arnoldiana
Arnold Flowering Crabapple

Broad, spreading, small tree with arching branches, ultimately 15 to 20 feet tall and long-lived. Covered in spring with clouds of large fragrant pink flowers which fade to white as they age. Little yellow crab-apples in fall. Hardy below zero.

2166

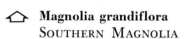 **Magnolia grandiflora**
Southern Magnolia

Evergreen with abundant, big, dark green, shiny leaves. In summer and fall, displays huge pearly-white blooms, which are intensely fragrant. The tree grows rather slowly, but will reach 60 feet in height with spread from 20 to 40 feet. Needs good drainage, plenty of moisture and responds to occasional feeding. Hardy to about 5 degrees above zero.

Liriodendron tulipifera
Tulip Tree

Tall, well-formed, deciduous tree, pyramidal to a height of 60 feet or more and spreads from 25 to 35 feet. Has big 4-lobed leaves of light bluish green, turning bright yellow in fall. In late spring, displays masses of tulip-like blooms of yellow and orange. Needs deep soil, summer moisture. Hardy below zero.

LS664

LS663

LS665

Malus micromalus
KAIDO CRABAPPLE

A hybrid crabapple of Japanese origin, of upright, vase form, reaching about 20 feet in height with a spread to 15 feet. Flowers in early May are pink, about 1½ in. diameter, fragrant. Fruits small, reddish tinged, September-October. Hardy to about 10 degrees above zero.

2416

Metrosideros tomentosa
NEW ZEALAND CHRISTMAS TREE

A dense, rounded evergreen tree with many branches and large glossy leaves. Grows slowly to 40 feet, or more. In June and July nearly every branch is tipped with clusters of showy crimson flowers. Thrives in sea winds and salt spray. Hardy to about 20 degrees above zero.

Malus pumila 'Niedzwetzkyana'
RED VEIN CRABAPPLE

A bushy-headed small tree eventually 18-20 feet tall and nearly as wide. All parts of the plant, including wood and flesh of the large fruit, colored purple. Flowers in early May, large, single; fruits in October. Native of southwest Siberia; hardy to about 25 degrees below zero.

LS610

LS666

Oxydendrum arboreum
SOURWOOD; SORREL TREE

An excellent small tree both for its late flowering season (late July-August) and outstanding fall leaf color (late October-early November). Habit upright and compact, growing rather slowly to about 40 feet with a spread of 25 feet. Flowers small, white, in panicles, resembling those of Pieris (Andromeda); the peach-like leaves change to bright red or scarlet and usually last two weeks or more. Hardy to zero.

2359

Olea europaea
COMMON OLIVE

Picturesque round-headed, bushy, evergreen tree, slow growing to about 25 feet. Has gray bark, long, dull, green leaves which are silvery beneath, and fruit varying by variety. Grows readily in most soils and is very drought resistant. Hardy to about 10 degrees above zero.

Morus alba 'Stribling'
STRIBLING MULBERRY

Fast-growing, broadly round-headed, deciduous shade tree, dense with large handsome foliage. Grows to about 35 feet. Desirable because of its lack of fruit and its ability to thrive in most any soil. Resists heat, alkali and neglect. Hardy below zero.

LS667

Butia capitata
PINDO PALM
Syn. *Cocos australis*

This sturdy palm is hardy to about 15 degrees, thrives in severe heat and can survive prolonged droughts. Relatively slow growth to a height of 15 to 20 feet with a spread of 10 to 15 feet.

LS265

Cycas revoluta
SAGO PALM

Botanically not a palm, but has been associated with them for many years. It is of the Cycad family. *Cycas revoluta* with its stout trunk and thick cluster of dark green fronds, finely divided, seldom exceeds a height of 10 ft. after years of growth. Used principally where taller plants are undesirable and in planter boxes and tubs. Needs considerable moisture and will thrive in full sun or semi-shade. Hardy to about 15 degrees.

Arecastrum romanzoffianum
QUEEN PALM
Syn. *Cocos plumosa*

Excellent for group plantings where tropical effect is desired in home gardens, around commercial buildings, pools and parks. Its growth is moderately rapid, forming a tree to 20 to 30 feet with slender trunk and graceful arching fronds. Is hardy to about 25 degrees under most conditions although young tender trees may freeze at a warmer temperature. Requires ample supply of water and sunshine.

LS668

LS669

Phoenix reclinata
SENEGAL DATE PALM ⇨

Resembles graceful coconut palm of South Seas. Generally forms several slender trunks by branching from the ground, but can be trained to form a single trunk. Thrives in full sun or semi-shade, withstanding temperatures as low as 20 degrees. Semi-rapid growth to 15 or 20 feet. Requires considerable moisture.

LS670

2373

Erythea edulis
GUADALUPE PALM

Withstands hot summer sun and winter temperatures to about 25 degrees. Sturdy trunk requires little cleaning because leaf stems drop clean. Reaches a height of 15 to 30 feet. Thrives in most areas of California except deserts. Most beautiful in spring when colorful clusters of golden blooms contrast with bright green foliage.

Washingtonia robusta
MEXICAN FAN PALM ⇨

Well suited to group planting in home and commercial gardens. Fairly rapid growth to 60 or 80 feet and retains some old foliage forming a petticoat effect just below green foliage. Hardy to about 15 degrees.

LS671

LS672

Prunus amygdalus 'Pendula'
WEEPING FLOWERING ALMOND

A very showy tree in spring when pink flowers form. Rapid growth in early stages and eventually reaching about 25 feet in height and spread. Hardy to about 5 degrees above zero.

LS673

Platanus occidentalis
AMERICAN SYCAMORE

Deciduous shade tree which grows rapidly to 80 feet or more, with a spread up to 60 feet. Has large, light green, maple-like leaves and sheds old bark in sections to expose new white bark on trunk and branches. Hardy below zero.

Pittosporum undulatum ⇨
VICTORIAN BOX

Large shrub or may be trained as a small, densely foliaged, round-headed, evergreen tree to about 25 feet with a spread of 15 to 20 feet. Has long, dark green, 6-inch, undulating leaves. Fragrant creamy-white blossoms in spring are followed by small orange-colored fruits. Hardy to about 20 degrees above zero.

2360

LS674

Prunus cerasifera 'Thundercloud'
FLOWERING PLUM

A small tree growing to height and spread of 25 feet at a medium rate. Bears pink flowers in spring. Leaves a rich red gradually turning darker red. Hardy to zero.

LS675

Prunus blireiana
FLOWERING PLUM

A hybrid flowering plum tree somewhat smaller and more graceful in habit than the well known purple-leaf plum. Grows 20 to 25 feet high, with a spread of 15 to 20 feet. In spring before the red-bronze foliage appears the branches are lined with showy double pink flowers. Full sun for best foliage color. Hardy below zero.

Prunus cerasifera 'Pissardi'
PURPLE-LEAF PLUM

Distinctive purple-red foliage. Grows rather erectly in fan-like form to 20 or 25 feet, with a spread of 15 to 20 feet. Many little, single, pinkish-white flowers are displayed against the dark red of the opening leaf buds each spring. Grows in almost any soil. Hardy below zero.

LS676

LS677

Prunus persica
FLOWERING PEACH

One of the best of spring flowering trees for mild-wintered areas. This tree rarely grows to 25 feet high or spreads to 20 feet. Available in a range of colors and variegations from white to deep red. Several new varieties produce fine edible fruit in addition to flowers. Hardy to zero.

2125

Prunus serrulata 'Kwanzan'
ORIENTAL CHERRY

A rather upright tree which grows rapidly to about 20 feet, with equivalent spread. Each spring the branches are lined solidly with masses of bloom — very double 2-inch flowers of deep rose-pink. Best in cool moist areas. One of the hardiest — to zero degrees.

Prunus persica 'Rubro-plena'
DOUBLE RED FLOWERING PEACH

A garden show piece each spring when every branch is crowded with big double flowers of rich red. This tree has been known to grow to 25 feet high and spread to 20 feet. Should be pruned rather severely at the end of the blooming season to make the new wood on which next season's bloom will appear. Hardy to zero.

LS678

Prunus triloba 'Multiplex'
FLOWERING ALMOND

This variety is usually a shrub but can be grown as a small tree reaching a height and spread of 10 feet. Bears double pink flowers in spring before leaves appear. Hardy to about zero. Rather slow growing.

LS679

LS130

Prunus serrulata 'Kiku-shidare-zakura'
WEEPING CHERRY

Pendulous form of Japanese cherry, usually grafted or budded to form standard tree. Flowers very double, pink, freely produced in May. Prefers cool climates and some winter cold. Hardy to about zero.

Prunus serrulata 'Shiro-fugen'
DOUBLE WHITE FLOWERING CHERRY

Grows 15 to 20 feet tall and rather spreading. Its spread is about equal to its height as a mature tree. Has large double flowers which open soft pink, changing to white. Bloom is profuse, the tree becoming a mass of flowers. New foliage appearing as the blossoms fade is bronzy-green. Fast growing tree, hardy to 5 degrees above zero.

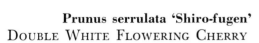

LS680

LS681

1923

Pyrus kawakami
EVERGREEN PEAR

May be used as a large shrub, a small tree, or is excellent grown in espalier fashion. Will reach height of 15 feet and spread to 15 feet. The shiny foliage is fresh looking and attractive all year. In spring has fragrant single white pear blossoms. Grows rapidly and easily but grafted plants bloom best. Hardy to about 18 degrees.

Prunus yedoensis 'Akebono'
YOSHINO CHERRY

Grows to a large tree of 30 feet tall with a spread of 20 feet. Blooms early, the bare branches being covered each spring with single light pink blooms fading white. Most of the famous flowering cherries of Washington, D.C., are of this species of which Akebono is one of the best forms. Hardy to about 5 degrees and one of the longest lived of the Japanese Cherries.

2279

LS327

Quercus agrifolia
CALIFORNIA LIVE OAK

Picturesque, round-headed, evergreen oak, densely clothed with spiny, polished, dark green leaves. Will reach 50 feet or more in height and as much in diameter. Does well almost everywhere except dry desert sections. Needs moisture and good drainage. Hardy to about 12 degrees.

LS648

Quercus coccinea
SCARLET OAK

Probably the best large tree for fall color effect. More open branching habit than the pin or red oaks but less easy to transplant. Height 60-70 feet and spread 45-50 feet. Prefers sandy or gravelly soils and well-drained sites. Hardy to about 15 degrees below zero.

LS682

Robinia hispida
ROSE-ACACIA LOCUST

May be a free-branching 7- or 8-foot shrub, or, trained as a small tree, will reach 10 or 12 feet, with spread equal to height. Has soft green, fern-like foliage and in May and June drooping clusters of sweetpea-like flowers, rose-pink in color. Easily grown in any soil. Hardy below zero.

2374

Quercus ilex
HOLLY OAK

A handsome evergreen oak with a compact rounded head, which grows moderately fast to about 40 or 50 feet and spreads to 50 feet when mature. The leaves are holly-like, dark green and glossy. Makes an excellent street tree, behaving well under widely varying conditions of soil and climate. Hardy to about 18 degrees.

Salix babylonica
WEEPING WILLOW

A medium sized deciduous shade tree growing to 30 or 40 feet high and spreading from 50 to 70 feet, long pendulous branches hanging to the ground. Narrow, bright green leaves are abundant, giving the tree a dense look. A feature of the gardens of Babylon and well-known throughout the world. Easily grown almost anywhere. Hardy to zero.

LS489

LS683

Tamarix parviflora
TAMARISK

Large shrub or small tree with reddish bark and slender branches covered with needle-like foliage. Grows irregularly to a height of about 15 feet. In early summer displays many feathery spikes of tiny pink flowers. Thrives almost anywhere, standing heat, drought and alkali. Hardy to about 15 degrees.

Sorbus aucuparia   LS649
EUROPEAN MOUNTAIN ASH

A dense, round-headed to pyramidal deciduous tree which will average about 30 feet in height with a spread of 15 to 20 feet. Many white spring flowers are followed by bright orange berries. Grows quite fast, but needs winter cold for blossoms and berries. Hardy below zero.

Schinus terebinthifolia
BRAZILIAN PEPPER-TREE

A neat round-headed evergreen tree, densely foliaged — 20 to 25 feet tall, with a spread of 20 feet. In fall displays showy scarlet berries. An excellent small tree for parkway or lawn. Grows easily with no special care. Hardy to about 22 degrees.

2372

Ulmus parvifolia sempervirens
EVERGREEN CHINESE ELM

A small tree with a spreading crown of bright green foliage. The best selected strains will seldom exceed 25 feet in height and spread, and will have a graceful semi-weeping habit. Practically evergreen but may drop leaves for a short while in coldest sections. Hardy to about 10 degrees.

2294

2293

Ulmus pumila
SIBERIAN ELM

Grows rapidly to 30 or 40 feet and may eventually reach 60 feet or more in height with a spread up to 50 feet. Hardy to 15 or 20 degrees below zero, and will succeed in dry areas, but branches are frequently broken by ice storms. Leaves are small and the habit rather open.

Zelkova serrata
JAPANESE ZELKOVA, or KEAKI

An elegant large tree related to the elms, eventually reaching 70-80 feet and forming a broad, spreading head to 70-80 feet. Leaves narrow, pointed and sharply toothed, changing to russet red in fall. Resistant to Dutch elm disease and recommended as a substitute for American elm. Hardy to about zero.

LS685

DECIDUOUS FLOWERING SHRUBS

Section 20

DECIDUOUS FLOWERING SHRUBS

Introduction

OF ALL THE TYPES of plants customarily planted around the home grounds, none yield as great a return of beautiful flowers and foliage for a very modest cost as do the deciduous flowering shrubs. Most of them are remarkably tolerant of poor soil and adverse growing conditions and there is a wide selection of varieties available, some of which will thrive in sub-tropical regions, many in the temperate areas of the country, and others under the harshest climatic conditions. There is some overlapping between the shrubs and smaller flowering trees, as some shrubs grow to be very large indeed at maturity. In general, however, deciduous shrubs are multi-stemmed woody plants which at maturity are from two or three feet to twelve to fifteen feet tall. Most of them grow at least as broad as tall and many are considerably broader. Most of the varieties illustrated are entirely deciduous and shed their leaves in the fall months, although a few like the buddleias and *Viburnum burkwoodi* are almost evergreen in mild climates. A few like the Carolina jessamine and the climbing hydrangea are vines, but can also be trimmed and grown in shrub form.

The largest number of our garden deciduous shrubs belong to that wide-spread tribe which occupies so much of the temperate zone — the rose family *(Rosaceae)*. Every gardener is familiar with its characteristic or "type" member the rose, but not all realize that such seemingly dissimilar groups as the spireas, quinces, cherries, kerrias, ocean spray, and bush cinquefoils *(Potentilla)* are also members. All have alternately arranged leaves, usually showy flowers with stamens in multiples of 5, and they thrive in the home grounds.

Another very important group of garden shrubs is included in the honeysuckle family *(Caprifoliaceae)*. In addition to our bush and climbing honeysuckles, such irreplaceable groups as the viburnums, weigelas and beauty bush are members of this useful tribe. All have leaves arranged in opposite pairs, and many have colorful berries which give a second season of interest after the flowers have passed.

Many of our most prized shrubs are included in the olive family *(Oleaceae)*, among them such favorites as the lilacs, forsythias and such useful hedge plants as the privets. The leaves are usually oppo-

Deciduous Flowering Shrubs (Continued)

sitely arranged and although the fruits are often inconspicuous, the spectacular spring flowers in this group form some of our finest garden displays.

The fourth big family of important deciduous shrubs is the saxifrage family *(Saxifragaceae)* which among others includes such colorful spring and summer bloomers as the mock-oranges, deutzias, and hydrangeas. They are widely planted for their spectacular floral displays and tolerance of difficult growing conditions. The other flowering shrubs illustrated are included in many diverse families which cannot be described within the limitations of this volume, but all have been selected for their outstanding flowers or foliage, or both.

Landscaping

Like any other group of plants, the deciduous flowering shrubs are well adapted to certain uses in the home landscape and are not suitable for others. Any residential community will show many examples of proper and improper planting. Their very modest cost has induced many "beginner" gardeners to plant them in situations to which they are not suited and the subsequent disappointment and the neces-

sity of removing them has sometimes given them unwarranted disfavor. All of this lost time and effort can be avoided at the beginning if the home owner will bear in mind certain general principles which are suggested below.

The first suggestion concerns so called "foundation planting" around the immediate periphery of the house itself. One should recognize at the start that many shrubs are so vigorous and large that they can be kept small enough for foundation use only by harsh pruning which destroys their beauty and necessitates much unnecessary work with the shears. Such plants as forsythias, Pee Gee hydrangea, kolkwitzia, magnolias, bush honeysuckles and Van Houtte spirea, to name a few, are too robust for this purpose. However, many of the dwarf growing types such as the dwarf quinces, slender and Lemoine deutzias, bush cinquefoil, pink flowering almond, Anthony Waterer spirea, and Eva Rathke weigela can be very tastefully combined with broadleaf and coniferous evergreens and will do much to brighten up the foundation planting during their various seasons of bloom. They create a much finer effect if planted in groups of three or five together rather than as in-

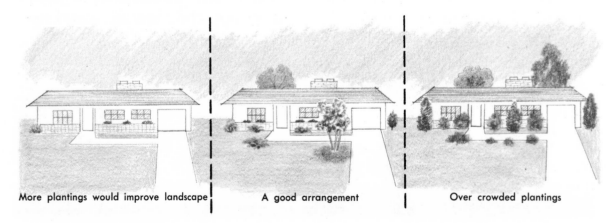

More plantings would improve landscape | A good arrangement | Over crowded plantings

Deciduous Flowering Shrubs (Continued)

dividuals or strung out in a straight line along the wall of the house. Such groups can be tied in with the rest of the foundation planting (and much cultivating avoided) if they are underplanted with an evergreen ground cover such as pachysandra or English ivy. There is also often a place for a single large specimen shrub of unusual interest as a feature plant near a corner of the house or adjoining a terrace area, perhaps underplanted with harmonizing broadleaf evergreens and ground cover plants. Such an accent point is frequently used with houses of contemporary or informal design and may terminate an extension of the foundation planting into the yard itself. A winged euonymus, crapemyrtle, magnolia, lilac clump, or viburnum is excellent for such a use.

The stronger growing shrubs are ideal for forming a border planting, en masse, to screen and give privacy to outdoor living areas in the back yard. They form a beautiful back drop for the flower garden, dining area, swimming pool, or children's play area and attract birds to the yard as well. Here again, plantings of larger groups of a few harmonizing varieties with varying seasons of bloom give a better effect than one each of a great number of individual varieties. Such mass plantings can also be used to break up the yard into special areas for special purposes and thus greatly increase its utility at a very modest cost.

Last of all, deciduous shrubs are ideal for clipped hedges or informal flowering ones. Privet and barberry have been used for many years as formal, clipped hedges. The winged euonymus is now becoming extremely popular for this purpose, too.

Although the initial cost is a bit higher, the plant grows only once a year and hence needs but one trimming a year to keep it perfectly neat. Furthermore, the fall foliage is a wonderful rosy red, and the corky-winged twigs give an effective visual barrier all through the winter. Several varieties are ideal as informal flowering hedges which need never be trimmed at all. They are planted at eighteen or twenty-four inch intervals for tall growing hedge types such as red honeysuckle, bridal wreath spirea, beauty bush, forsythia, lilacs, or Vanicek weigela. The dwarf deutzias and Anthony Waterer spirea make splendid, low, flowering hedges not exceeding two or three feet in height. Plant them about twelve inches apart. The beauty of one of these informal flowering hedges of a suitable species has to be seen to be believed.

Culture

Unlike some of the specialty plants, deciduous shrubs are a delight to the beginning gardener as well as the more experienced one because of the ease with which entirely satisfactory results can be achieved. Most of them are easy to transplant and are not exacting in their soil requirements. They will thrive in either moderately acid, neutral, or moderately alkaline soils of average fertility although, like any other plant, they benefit from extra care taken in soil preparation and from an annual light fertilizing. Since many lots, especially in the newer developments, have been carelessly leveled and regraded by the bulldozer, and since the soil excavated from the cellar hole (if there is one) is often simply spread about as near as possible to the house itself, it

Deciduous Flowering Shrubs (Continued)

pays to take some extra pains in preparing the actual planting holes. The average two- to three-foot or three- to four-foot shrub should have a hole dug approximately twelve inches deep and eighteen inches wide to receive it. The soil removed should be thoroughly mixed with about a third to one-fourth of humus or peat moss (by volume) and a cup of commercial fertilizer and then piled beside the hole.

If the plant has been received "bare root," or with roots wrapped in moss or some similar substance, the wrappings should be removed and the roots soaked in a pail of water for some minutes. This measure is unnecessary if the plant was container grown or received "balled and burlapped" with a ball of soil in which it was grown still intact around the roots. In either case the plant is placed in the hole at the same depth at which it grew in the nursery. Then the soil mix piled beside the hole is gently shoveled back in around the roots, shaking the bare root plant gently from time to time to work the loose soil well into and around the root mass. Then the soil is tamped in firmly (but not stamped or pounded hard) to anchor the plant and to eliminate air pockets which would allow the roots to dry out. The remaining soil is formed into a little circular ridge around the planting hole thus making it a shallow "bowl." Finally

this bowl is filled with water several times and allowed to soak gently into the soil. A mulch of pine needles, salt hay, leaves or peat will prevent rapid drying out in the sun and wind and greatly increase the benefits from each watering.

Newly planted shrubs should be watered thoroughly, once a week if there is no rain, until they are well leafed out and established. They should be pruned back at planting time to one-half their height if they were not previously trimmed by the seller. This seems a harsh measure, but the rapid and vigorous regrowth which results will more than justify it. Deciduous shrubs, like small coniferous and broadleaf evergreens, ordinarily do not need any staking after planting. The only exceptions to this rule are shrubs grown in standard or "tree" form such as tree wisterias, tree hydrangeas and tree hibiscus which are somewhat top-heavy and would otherwise be whipped and loosened by the wind until established in their new location.

Care In Subsequent Years

The shrubs illustrated in these pages have been selected in part because they do not require exacting yearly care. No weekly spraying or dusting program is necessary to control fungi as in the rose garden. The few insect pests which may occur

⅔ SOIL ⅓ PEAT 18" 12"

SOAK BARE ROOT PLANTS BEFORE PLANTING

MULCH OF PEAT OR LEAVES FILL BOWL WITH WATER SEVERAL TIMES

Deciduous Flowering Shrubs *(Continued)*

are largely aphids which sometimes appear on the new growth of spireas and a few other varieties. These are easily eliminated by a spraying with Malathion or Nicotine if they do seem to be troublesome. Fertilizing should be done in the spring when new growth starts, using about a tea cup full of a 1-1-1 or 1-2-1 ratio fertilizer per two-foot unit of shrub height. The fertilizer should be scratched into the ground with a cultivator or applied before the mulch is renewed if the plants are mulched.

Most of these shrubs are remarkably drouth resistant and do not require supplemental watering in areas of normal rainfall. In dry regions, where watering is necessary to maintain a lawn and shade trees, of course the shrubs must be watered, too. But this is a routine procedure in such places. During unusual summer drouths in otherwise normal areas the bigleaf hydrangeas and their French hybrids as well as Japanese snowballs and other viburnums may exhibit drooping leaves and signs of distress. At such times a good deep soaking is worth a dozen light sprinklings with the hose, and of course a thick, porous mulch will greatly reduce the necessity for watering.

The degree of hardiness of these shrubs is given in the descriptions accompanying each color plate. By checking the hardiness data and planting the varieties described as reliable in your particular area or in colder zones there will be no necessity for winter protection for deciduous shrubs. Although gardeners enjoy the challenge of growing plants not quite reliably hardy in their own area, common sense will dictate that there is no point in trying to grow Carolina yellow jessamine in Boston, crapemyrtle in Chicago, or poinsettia in Portland, for example. However, a little winter protection will bring somewhat tender varieties like the various butterfly bushes and French hydrangeas through the winter successfully in such areas as the inland portions of Zone 6 (see Zone Hardiness Map).

Although most gardeners soon become expert in soil preparation, planting, and fertilizing deciduous shrubs, many continue year after year to mar the beauty of their shrubs by improper pruning practices. This is simply the result of misinformation coupled with enthusiasm, and once the very simple principles are understood there is no more difficulty. A few suggestions with illustrative drawings are given below showing proper and improper pruning methods.

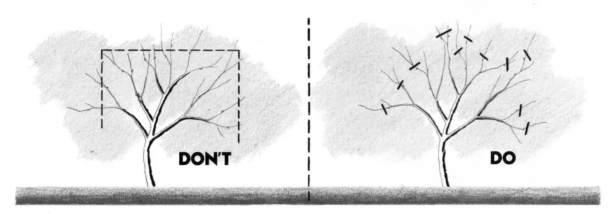

DON'T   DO

Deciduous Flowering Shrubs (Continued)

All hedges, whether composed of evergreen or deciduous plants, should be trimmed so that the base is a bit wider than the top (see below). The reason for this shape is that it allows enough light to strike the lower branches so that they continue to grow and put forth abundant foliage. The hedge trimmed wider at the top than the base, or with parallel sides, shades the lower branches to such a degree that they begin to thin out and do not produce enough foliage to make a thick, luxuriant base so that much of its beauty and utility is lost.

Those shrubs which bloom on branches which grow during the current year (and these are usually summer rather than spring bloomers) should be pruned in the spring before growth starts. If it is desired to keep them small, they can even be treated like herbaceous perennials and cut to the ground each spring and they will put on a fine show of bloom that summer.

CORRECT METHOD OF PRUNING HEDGE

Butterfly bush, hydrangeas, poinsettias, bush cinquefoil, and Anthony Waterer spirea are all in this class. Those shrubs which bloom on "old wood" or branches formed the summer before should be pruned as soon as they have finished blooming. This makes it possible to enjoy the flowers and still trim back the shrub early enough for it to recover and fill out nicely, forming abundant blooming wood for the following spring's display. Almost all of the other shrubs illustrated belong in this second class. In pruning these shrubs, they should not be simply clipped or "hedged" off into round or cylindrical shapes. This spoils their natural gracefulness and soon causes them to become thin and unsightly at the base. It is a much better plan to cut out close to the ground the tallest and oldest woody shoots and leave the young vigorous ones to grow. If these shoots need shortening to reduce the overall size of the shrub, they should be cut at varying heights to preserve a graceful and natural appearance.

By using some thought in selecting the best shrubs for the purposes desired and satisfying their moderate requirements, the home grounds can be made outstandingly beautiful at very little expense and effort. No other class of garden plants gives a greater yield of beauty and utility for so small an investment. The color plates and descriptions which follow will be most helpful in choosing the varieties best suited to your needs from this useful group of plants.

Berberis thunbergi atropurpurea
PURPLE LEAVED JAPANESE BARBERRY

This form of the well known Japanese barberry is valuable for its purple leaf color in summer, changing to deep red in October; the compact habit makes it excellent for hedges 3 to 5 feet in height. Hardy to 5 to 10 degrees below zero.

LS826

Buddleia davidi magnifica
FOUNTAIN BUTTERFLY BUSH

An excellent shrub for summer effect, being at its peak in July and August, and easily propagated by seeds or cuttings. There are now numerous color variations, from white through pink, lavender, and purple to near red. Bushes should be pruned hard annually in March. A native of China. Hardy to about 5 degrees below zero.

LS827

Calycanthus floridus
CAROLINA ALLSPICE

Deciduous shrub growing to 10 feet in height and 6 to 8 feet in spread. Thrives in rich, well drained soil, bearing sweet-scented, reddish-brown flowers, April to August. Hardy to about zero degrees.

LS833

LS828

Chaenomeles lagenaria 'Sanguinea'
FLOWERING QUINCE

Stiff-branched, angular, deciduous shrub growing to about 6 feet in height, somewhat more in spread. In earliest spring breaks into bloom with long-lasting blood-red flowers lining each branch. Thrives in almost any soil and will stand heat or drought. Hardy to 5 degrees below zero.

LS829

**Chaenomeles lagenaria 'Alba';
'Appleblossom'; 'Atrococcinea'**
FLOWERING QUINCE

Generally 4 to 6 feet. Stiff irregular shrubs, more spreading than tall. Before the leaves appear, the plants break into bloom with long-lasting flowers lining each branch. Red, pink and white forms are available. Easily grown. Hardy to about 5 degrees below zero.

Chaenomeles lagenaria
PINK FLOWERING QUINCE

2395

Chaenomeles lagenaria
JAPANESE FLOWERING QUINCE

An early spring flowering shrub, variable in height, habit and flower color, but usually growing 5 to 8 feet tall. Flowers white, orange, pink, scarlet or blood red. May be trained against a wall or fence. Hardy to about 5 degrees below zero.

LS834

LS830

Cytisus praecox
CREAM BROOM

Compact shrub with bright green stems and foliage, growing from 4 to 6 feet tall with about the same spread. In spring, every branch is lined with strongly scented pea-like flowers of creamy yellow. Best in full sun and sandy soils. Hardy to about 10 degrees.

2261

Deutzia scabra
PRIDE OF ROCHESTER

Deciduous shrub with slender branches, growing fountain-like to about 4 feet in height and spreading gracefully to about 5 feet. Has attractive light green leaves and snowy-white flower clusters in May. Hardy to below zero.

Corylopsis sinensis
CHINESE WINTER HAZEL

With its large gray-green toothed foliage, this makes a handsome shrub from 8 to 12 feet tall. Particularly attractive in early spring, when it displays countless spikes of fragrant yellow blooms. Needs sun and good drainage. Hardy to about 10 degrees.

LS835

LS831

LS832

Daphne mezereum
FEBRUARY DAPHNE

A familiar and valuable 4 to 5 foot shrub from Europe and western Asia, one of the first to flower in spring (Feb.-March), colorful and most fragrant. The purple flowers are densely clustered up the stems and are followed by bright red berries in July. Tolerant of cold to about 15 degrees below zero.

Deutzia lemoinei
LEMOINE DEUTZIA

A very free-flowering and showy hybrid, growing 6 to 7 feet in height and blooming in June. Flowers in short panicles, white. Should be pruned annually after flowering. One of the hardiest deutzias, reliable to about 10 or 15 degrees below zero.

Euphorbia pulcherrima
POINSETTIA

Plant sends up tall "leggy" shoots to a height of 10 feet or more, to be crowned at the tips with the traditional Christmas flower of intense scarlet. Does best if cut back to 2 or 3 "eyes" after blooming. Likes full sun. Hardy to about 28 degrees.

LS575

LS543

Forsythia intermedia 'Spectabilis'
SHOWY FORSYTHIA, GOLDENBELLS

Of upright and arching habit, growing rapidly to 9 to 10 feet tall. Flowering freely late March to April, depending upon location. Golden yellow. Native of China. Hardy to 5 or 10 degrees below zero.

LS836

Euphorbia pulcherrima 'Mary Ecke'
DOUBLE POINSETTIA

Plant and habit the same as for *Euphorbia pulcherrima,* but flowers are high-centered and double with several rows of petals.

Euonymus alatus
WINGED EUONYMUS OR BURNING BUSH

The stiff, more or less horizontal branches are noticeably corky winged, hence the Latin and common names. Its most valuable characteristic is the brilliant crimson-red fall leaf color. Height and width about 8 feet. Native of northeast Asia, hardy to approximately 15 degrees below zero.

LS843

LS837

2131

Hibiscus syriacus
Shrub Althea

A large shrub, eventually reaching 10 to 12 feet in height, useful for its August blooming and variously-colored, single or double, conspicuous flowers, white, rose, carmine or blue-purple in hue. Hardiness limit to about 5 degrees below zero.

Hydrangea macrophylla
Bigleaf Hydrangea

Large, rounded shrub to 10 feet tall and 8 feet across. In June and July has heavy 8-inch panicles of white or pink flowers which turn blue when iron sulphate is added to the soil. Needs partial shade, plenty of moisture. Hardy to about 10 degrees.

Hydrangea macrophylla
Bigleaf Hydrangea

The color range of this hydrangea has been greatly extended by the "French hybrids." Deep tones of rose, carmine and red (below) are available, as are blue (below) and violet. Plants have same characteristics as the species, except that they may be more dwarf.

LS300

LS301

Hydrangea paniculata grandiflora
Pee Gee Hydrangea

Generally an upright shrub 10 to 15 feet tall, but can be trained as a small tree to 18 or 20 feet, with a spread of 8 or 10 feet. Blooms for many weeks in late summer, displaying many long panicles of white flowers, turning to rose or purplish as they age. Hardy to zero.

LS839

LS838

Hydrangea arborescens grandiflora
Hills of Snow

A native American shrub, grows 3 to 4 feet tall. Prefers partial shade and a soil with plenty of humus. Flowers mid-June to July, white, in large rounded clusters, very showy. Hardiness range to about 5 degrees below zero.

Kolkwitzia amabilis
Beauty Bush

A graceful, arching, deciduous Chinese shrub from 6 to 8 feet tall and as much across. In June every branch becomes a plume of little pink-and-orange flowers packed tightly together. Stands heat or wind and is hardy to about 10 degrees below zero.

LS844

Kerria japonica 'Pleniflora'
DOUBLE KERRIA

One of the few double yellow-flowered shrubs available, reaching 5 to 6 feet in height and flowering in May. The slender green stems are quite conspicuous in winter. Should be given a sunny but not too dry position. Native of China. Will withstand freezing to about 5 degrees below zero.

LS842

LS840

Lagerstroemia indica
CRAPEMYRTLE
Pink-flowered form of Crapemyrtle.

Lagerstroemia indica
CRAPEMYRTLE

Deciduous small tree or large shrub 10 to 25 feet tall, 10 to 12 feet in spread. In midsummer every branch is tipped with crinkly crepe-like flowers in large spikes. Flowers are white, lavender, pink or red according to variety. Blooms best inland. Hardy to about 15 degrees.

LS841

LS845

Ligustrum vulgare
COMMON PRIVET

This quick-growing, easily propagated shrub, of upright and densely branched habit, is frequently used for hedges, especially in Europe. The strongly scented panicles of white flowers appear in midsummer; the small black fruits usually remain until early spring. Will stand temperatures down to about 15 degrees below zero.

Magnolia liliflora
LILY MAGNOLIA

Deciduous shrub or little tree to 10 or 12 feet tall, with equivalent spread. For many weeks in spring the plant displays spectacular big purple and cream-colored lily-like flowers. Needs sun and good soil. Hardy to 5 or 10 degrees.

LS853

Lonicera korolkowi zabeli
BLUE-LEAF HONEYSUCKLE

Large deciduous shrub with soft blue-green foliage, which grows from 10 to 12 feet tall and somewhat less in spread. A profusion of small rose to pale pink flowers in May and June is followed by showy bright red fruits. Hardy to below zero degrees.

2503

LS846

Magnolia soulangeana
SAUCER MAGNOLIA

Good looking large shrub or small tree with bright green foliage. It grows irregularly to 8 or 10 feet tall with about the same spread. In early spring, before the leaves appear, giant cup-like blooms of creamy white and delicate pink adorn each branch. They are as fragrant as they are spectacular. Needs full sun. Hardy to about 5 degrees.

LS26

Magnolia stellata
STAR MAGNOLIA

A dwarf magnolia, 8 to 10 feet tall, spreading to 12 feet or more. It blooms early in the spring, becoming a mass of 3-inch wide, fragrant flowers, each with 12 or more snowy-white petals in a star-like arrangement. Needs good soil and moisture. Hardy to about 10 degrees.

LS538

LS847

LS848

Paeonia suffruticosa
TREE PEONY
Syn. *P. Moutan*

Rather open shrub with twisting branches and large-lobed leaves of blue-green tinted with bronze. It grows slowly to 5 or 6 feet tall, slightly less in spread. In late spring flowers often 12 inches across, which may be white, pink or red in color, are borne in profusion. Hardy below zero.

Philadelphus cymosus
MOCK ORANGE

A strong, fast-growing, deciduous shrub reaching fountain-like to 6 or 8 feet and spreading as much. One of late spring's most beautiful shrubs when covered with its clusters of very fragrant creamy-white flowers. Easily grown. Hardy to zero.

LS852

Philadelphus virginalis 'Virginal'
MOCK ORANGE

One of the most showy and fragrant double-flowered hybrids, blooming in June and growing 8 to 9 feet tall. The habit of the plant is leggy and the base should be hidden behind other shrubs. Originated in France over fifty years ago. Tolerates about 5 degrees below zero.

LS850

LS849

Philadelphus cymosus 'Atlas'
MOCK ORANGE

One of the most decorative of the single-flowered, pure white hybrid mock oranges, introduced by Lemoine of France in 1924. Height, 6 to 8 feet. Hardy to about 5 degrees below zero.

Philadelphus lemoinei 'Belle Etoile'
LEMOINE MOCK ORANGE

For habit, free flowering quality, and fragrance this is among the choicest of its race. The white, bowl-shaped flowers have a purplish stain inside. Height, 7 to 8 feet. Hardy to around 10 degrees below zero.

LS851

Prunus glandulosa 'Rosea Plena'
DOUBLE PINK FLOWERING ALMOND

A small, compact blooming shrub, reaching about 4 feet in height, producing many attractive pink flowers along the branches in April. Fruits are like small cherries in July. Hardy to about 15 degrees below zero.

LS854

LS445

Potentilla fruticosa 'Gold Drop'
SHRUBBY CINQUEFOIL

This is a low-growing, hardy, compact little shrub with golden yellow flowers in May. Its habit makes it suitable for rock gardens or banks, or to associate with or replace heathers. Tough enough for 35 to 40 degrees below zero.

Prunus jacquemonti
JACQUEMONT CHERRY

A fast-growing deciduous shrub, bushy, rounded and compactly foliaged, growing 8 to 10 feet tall and as much across. Single rose-colored blooms in spring are followed by good crops of little red edible cherries, ripening in May and June. Hardy to zero.

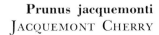

1556

Punica granatum 'Legrelle'
POMEGRANATE

A form of the pomegranate with double, white-striped, scarlet flowers, blooming for a long period in summer. In cool climates needs a south or west wall or fence behind it for shelter and warmth. Height up to 12 feet. Hardy to about 5 degrees, with some protection.

LS856

LS855

Spiraea bumalda 'Anthony Waterer'
ANTHONY WATERER SPIREA

One of the most useful smaller spireas, producing flat heads of rosy-crimson flowers, mid-June to early July. Should be planted in the front of groups or borders. It grows to 2 feet in height. Will stand about 5 degrees below zero.

Spiraea prunifolia plena
DOUBLE BRIDAL WREATH SPIREA

The double form of this 8-foot shrub from eastern Asia is superior to the single-flowered type; season late April to mid-May. The narrow leaves often color orange in fall. Will endure about 15 degrees below zero.

LS244

Spiraea thunbergi
THUNBERG SPIREA

An upright, slender-branched shrub of about 4 feet in height. Flowers white, in small umbels along the branches, March to April. Foliage small and narrow, sometimes coloring yellow or orange in fall. Tolerates cold to about 15 degrees below zero.

LS858

LS857

Syringa persica
PERSIAN LILACS IN PLANTING

A vigorous form with graceful, arching branches reaching to 8 feet in height and spread. Showy clusters of pale lavender fragrant flowers in late spring. Excellent for screenings. Hardy to zero.

Syringa vulgaris hybrids
DOUBLE WHITE LILAC

Recommended varieties of these handsome and fragrant May-flowering shrubs include 'Edith Cavell,' 'Ellen Willmott' and the old 'Mme. Lemoine.' All are hardy to 15 or 20 degrees below zero.

LS859

Syringa vulgaris
COMMON LILAC

The eastern lilac with its sweet-scented lavender-blue bloom in early spring makes a large shrub or small tree, 15 to 20 feet with a 10 foot spread. Many hybrids extend the range of flower colors from pure white to deep purple. These lilacs need winter cold to produce good bloom. All are hardy below zero.

LS609

LS20

Syringa vulgaris
FRENCH HYBRID LILAC

A deciduous shrub or small tree reaching 12 or more feet in height with a spread of 8 feet. These hybrids produce a wide range of flower colors in both double and single form. Most varieties are hardy below zero.

Viburnum burkwoodi
BURKWOOD VIBURNUM

A semi-deciduous shrub, handsomely foliaged, which grows 4 to 6 feet tall and 6 to 7 feet across. In early spring every branch bears clusters of pink-flushed white flowers with an intense gardenia-like fragrance. Best in partial shade. Hardy to zero.

LS860

LS862

Viburnum tomentosum sterile
JAPANESE SNOWBALL

A beautiful deciduous flowering shrub with large, ribbed, dark green leaves, becoming mahogany red in October. It grows about 8 feet tall, spreading as much or more. In June it is covered with perfectly globular 3- to 4-inch flower heads of snowy-white. Hardy to zero degrees.

LS439

Viburnum carlesi
KOREANSPICE VIBURNUM

The principal value of this hardy Korean species lies in its very fragrant clusters of white flowers in late April or early May. A partially shaded location is advisable; it may be attacked by leaf-curling aphis unless sprayed early. Height 5 to 6 feet. Will endure about 5 degrees below zero.

LS863

Weigela florida
PINK WEIGELA

Weigela florida 'Variegated'
GOLDEN LEAVED WEIGELA

Weigela 'Eva Rathke'
RED WEIGELA

The Weigelas are useful shrubs, upright in habit, averaging about 5 feet in height, somewhat less in spread. They are famous for the lavish show of trumpet-like flowers (white, pink and red by variety) appearing for many weeks in spring and early summer. Easily grown and hardy to zero degrees.

LS866

LS865

Weigela 'Vanicek'
VANICEK WEIGELA

Somewhat smaller than other varieties, growing to about 3 feet in height. The blooms appear late and continue over a long period, often into autumn. The flowers are large and showy. Prefers full sun. Hardy to zero.

Zenobia pulverulenta
DUSTY ZENOBIA

Graceful deciduous or semi-evergreen shrub with arching branches clothed with silvery foliage. It grows 3 to 4 feet in height and about the same in spread. Many showy little bell-shaped white flowers, 25 or more to a cluster, adorn the plant in May and June. Hardy to about 5 degrees.

LS867

BROADLEAVED EVERGREEN SHRUBS

Section 30

BROADLEAVED EVERGREEN SHRUBS

Introduction

THE TERM, broadleaved evergreen shrubs, is effective in setting this valuable group of plant materials apart from the coniferous evergreens with their needle- or scale-like leaves, and from deciduous shrubs which lose their leaves in winter. The foliage of the true evergreen persists for more than one full annual cycle and frequently for several years.

There are several classes of broadleaf evergreens. They may be separated according to their primary functions as foliage plants or flowering plants or as producers, predominantly, of berries or fruits.

Esthetic quality may form a basis for separation. Is a natural setting most suitable for a given plant, or does it have formality or else a boldness and lushness that suggest a tropical setting? Size of leaves can be extremely important in landscaping. In limited areas the use of large, bold foliage produces a crowded effect while small, neat foliage gives an impression of space and is in better scale with the surroundings.

Then there are cultural considerations. Some shrubs demand rich loamy soils, others prefer poor sandy ones. Some demand sun and others insist upon shade. Most succeed in a neutral soil but many fail unless an acid medium is provided. Regular pruning is essential in the production of good flowers in some species, while others rarely need this attention.

Let us take some of the selections illustrated on the following pages of this section and see how they fit the subdivision described above.

Few of the selections are purely foliage plants although several depend mostly on leaf beauty with an added bonus of interesting flowers or fruits. *Euonymus japonicus* 'Aureus' and *Fatsia japonica* are foliage plants only, while *Arbutus unedo, Ligustrum japonicum, Melianthus major, Nandina domestica* and *Pieris forresti* are examples of the bonus plants.

The major portion of the list is famous for its lovely flowers and to see *Ceanothus impressus* or *Cistus purpureus* in full bloom is to want it for your own. Beauty of berry is the attribute of the cotoneasters and pyracanthas while *Aucuba japonica* and *Skimmia japonica* produce lovely berries if a male plant is present for pollination. They also have attractive foliage.

It is well to bear in mind that while a shrub may be extremely beautiful in flower or berry, the peak of beauty is usually of short duration. For the balance of the year it must depend on the foliage alone, so it is important to choose the structural elements of our plantings for the values of the leaf and habit rather than for this short-term floral excellence alone.

The esthetic suitabilities of a shrub are harder to define and usually are determined by the experience, feeling or preference of the gardener. Most agree that *Kalmia latifolia* and the *Pieris* species are most happily placed in an informal setting or in a wild garden. Bold foliage is usually associated with the lushness of the tropics so the *Aralia, Aucuba, Crotalaria, Acanthus* and *Melianthus* are widely used to suggest a tropical atmosphere.

Broadleaved Evergreen Shrubs (Continued)

Landscaping

The preceding remarks provide some hints that can be applied to the use of these important shrubs in the garden. However, there are millions of new home owners who from choice or from financial necessity do most of their own planning and planting. They have not yet attained the level of experience that provides the "feeling" for individual plants that would indicate proper placing in the garden.

For those who want a well balanced and well designed garden, plants should be regarded as units only of the complete plan. It is more important that each individual tree and shrub become a part of the over-all plan than that it have outstanding characteristics. This does not mean that one must settle for common or drab materials. The plants may be new and sparkling if properly blended into the design.

The novice gardener, and many experienced ones, would do well to compare their gardens to some other familiar pattern. Consider, if you will, the garden as an outdoor room or series of rooms. Then consider the elements that produce a lovely interior room. No matter how charming a room may be, with pleasantly tinted walls, beautiful rugs and even elegant drapes, it is not complete without furniture. This is further enhanced by the addition of lamps, pictures, pillows and books. The furniture is still the dominant influence in the room and tends to hold the basic plan together.

Let us turn back to the garden. In addition to the fences that form the boundaries, you have chosen, from other chapters in this book, the trees and conifers that become the walls of your garden room. The lawns and ground-cover plants as well as paved or graveled areas are your carpet. The colorful features will be chosen later from the deciduous shrub list and the array of annuals, perennials and bulbs suitable for your area. This leaves the all-important items of furniture, the broadleaf evergreen and other shrubs.

INFORMAL LANDSCAPE
Avoid straight line plantings. Form bays to create illusion of greater depth and provide added protection for tender varieties

Broadleaved Evergreen Shrubs (Continued)

Choose your shrubs as you would your furniture. Plan to use several plants of the same variety and mass them in bold groups to give stability to the design. A large group in one area should be repeated in a smaller group elsewhere. This permits the use of single specimens or smaller groups of contrasting varieties much as you would select a contrasting color for your occasional chair in the home. The massing of the shrubs used in the repeat pattern eliminates the "busy" or distracting effect of planting single specimens in a mixed or alternate plan.

Except in a perfectly balanced formal type of garden the broadleaf evergreen shrubs should never be planted in a straight line. Drift some of the taller varieties forward in the border and let some of the more dwarf groups run back in bays formed by larger plants. This prevents seeing all of the garden from a single vantage point and leads one on to new discoveries. It also has real value in providing more protection for the choicer varieties.

The most frequent mistake made by beginners and by far too many advanced gardeners is overplanting. The large majority of nursery stock is sold in gallon-can or equivalent size. Rarely are mature specimens growing in the nursery, and the novice has very little idea of the ultimate size. Reliable nurserymen never intentionally over-sell their customers but the temptation of all the beautiful plants on display is generally too strong for the gardener. The desire to have an immediate display overcomes caution and good advice and the result is overcrowding. This would be perfectly all right if the plants were thinned as they began to crowd each other but very few gardeners have the heart to do this. The alternative is a sad one; constant heavy pruning to keep the shrubs in their allotted space. This not only becomes a tedious and steadily growing task but robs the shrubs of their inherent characteristics and beauty.

Culture

PREPARATION OF THE SOIL

Most of the shrubs in the following pages of this chapter are relatively undemanding. Any good soil that supports a reasonable growth of other plant types will suit them well. Good soil preparation will pay dividends in added vigor and beauty. As shrubs usually remain permanently where they are planted it is only before planting that any improvement of existing conditions can be attained.

The most important condition to consider is drainage. If the soil is heavy and the sub-soil does not drain well it would be advisable to double trench the entire area where shrubs are to be grown. In extreme cases drain tile will be necessary to carry off excess water.

Should the soil be lacking in humus it would be well to spade in the most readily available material to improve the tilth of the soil. Leaf-mold, peat, stable manure or compost are used for this purpose. Sawdust or shavings may be used if additional nitrogen is provided to support the bacteria that decompose this material.

Some plants require an acid soil with a high humus content in order to survive. The rhododendrons and azaleas are well known examples but several shrubs in this listing also require an acid medium. The *Erica* or heath and *Calluna* or heather need

Broadleaved Evergreen Shrubs (Continued)

acid, peaty soil, as well as *Kalmia latifolia*, *Pieris japonica* and *P. forresti* and *Skimmia japonica*. If a soil test indicates a highly alkaline soil these plants should not be attempted.

PLANTING AND STAKING

The actual planting in a well prepared soil is a simple procedure but if the planting is done in holes dug in firm, compacted soil more labor is required. Dig the hole at least twice the size of the ball of roots. Some of the friable top soil should be put in the bottom of the hole and well firmed so that the weight of the plant will not cause it to settle. If plant is in a can or pot remove it carefully so the ball of earth will not be broken. If the root system appears to be pot bound it is well to slightly loosen the exterior of the ball. Balled and burlapped plants should be planted in the sacking and the sacking peeled back from the neck only after the shrub is placed and the hole three-fourths filled with loam. Lay a stick or tool handle across the hole to show the ground level so that the shrub can be placed at exactly the same depth as it was before. Some settling is inevitable; and deep planting is greatly resented by many shrubs, causing the death of countless rhododendrons.

The root mass at planting time should be in a well moistened condition, insured by a short immersion in a tub if there is any doubt about it. After planting, the loose soil returned to the hole should be well firmed so that good contact with the roots is obtained. Nurseries frequently grow plants in very firm soil so that they can be dug with good earth balls. If these earth balls are dry in the center, when planted in light, loamy, or sandy soils, all water will soak away from the balls and the plant will die of drought even though freely watered. A soil basin should remain around the plant for the first few weeks.

Staking is rarely necessary with broadleaf evergreens, but if a windy location whips the plant until an air space is worked around the collar, it would be well to provide a firm support. A short, sturdy stake is to be preferred to a tall whippy one, as all that is necessary to keep the lower stems secure. Tie loosely with soft material or run a wire through a short length of old garden hose and staple to the stake.

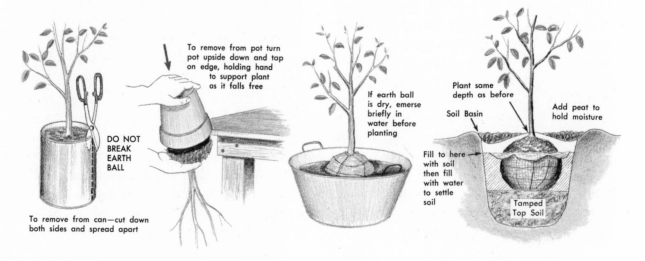

DO NOT BREAK EARTH BALL

To remove from can—cut down both sides and spread apart

To remove from pot turn pot upside down and tap on edge, holding hand to support plant as it falls free

If earth ball is dry, emerse briefly in water before planting

Plant same depth as before

Soil Basin

Add peat to hold moisture

Fill to here with soil then fill with water to settle soil

Tamped Top Soil

Broadleaved Evergreen Shrubs (Continued)

CARE AFTER PLANTING

A newly planted shrub should be watched carefully for the first few weeks and given adequate water to sustain it. Do not make the mistake of overwatering to the extent that the soil becomes soggy. It is better to lightly syringe the foliage frequently for the first few days to keep wilting to a minimum. If leaf flagging persists or is severe, it may be necessary to cut back the soft shoots to firmer wood. If hot, sunny weather occurs immediately after planting, it would be well to lightly shade the plant for a few days. Drying winds are especially harmful and should be screened off if possible. Avoid over-shading or over-protection, as the shrub may be encouraged to put out soft new growth which will be damaged as soon as the protection is removed.

WATERING

Frequency of watering depends on the exposure, soil conditions, weather conditions and season of the year as well as the variety involved. How to water is easier to define. Thoroughness is the secret of successful watering. Determine by test how much water is needed to penetrate your particular soil deeper than the root system. This will permit the roots to go down and provide insurance against the time when they must go for some time without water. Frequent light sprinklings cause the roots, by necessity, to come to the surface where they are easily injured by drought, freezing or cultivating. Less frequent deep watering permits air to enter the soil between irrigations and air is just as important to the root system as water. The use of overhead sprinklers is greatly appreciated by most shrubs and will materially discourage the attack of scale and red spider mite.

FERTILIZING

It is usually good practice to allow newly planted shrubs to become well established before a fertilizing program is started. If the soil is rich and has been well prepared with the addition of the materials listed under soil preparation, a year or more could elapse before fertilizing is necessary. Each area has a well known brand of fertilizer usually compounded for that particular region. Your nurseryman can provide this material and it should be used according to directions.

The acid soil plants should be fertilized only with products especially compounded for them as some products have an alkaline reaction harmful to this group. The use of a heavy mulch of leaf mold or pine needles, renewed once or twice a year, usually provides all the nutrients that ericaceous plants require.

PROTECTION

One of the valuable contributions of this volume is the inclusion of minimum temperatures at which each described tree or shrub can survive. The choice of plant materials for your garden should stay above this stated minimum in most if not all cases. Winter protection is a laborious, costly and unsightly endeavor when a great number of tender species are grown. Even the plants considered hardy in your area will sometimes severely "burn." This condition is not caused by the cold but by sudden changes in temperature. Sun and wind can dry out the leaves of evergreens while the roots are frozen and unable to supply the demand for moisture. To prevent this burning it is only necessary to build a windbreak of brush, burlap or lath to cut down transpiration of the leaves.

Broadleaved Evergreen Shrubs (Continued)

A heavy mulch of leaves or chips, strawy manure or other coarse materials will prevent alternate thawing and freezing.

PRUNING

Many of the shrubs in our list require very little pruning except for training and control. Of course broken, dead or crossing branches should be removed from all plants as soon as observed. If the shrubs were wisely chosen and properly spaced they may be allowed to attain the size and form that nature intended. Do not prune unless a definite need or reason requires it. More harm can be done by needless pruning than is generally realized. Above all do not use hedge shears for general pruning. They are meant for trimming hedges and formal plants such as boxwood. All gardeners should have a good pair of sturdy pruning shears and keep them in good condition. Sharp shears make clean cuts that look neat and heal rapidly.

Some of the broadleaved evergreens that are grown primarily for their flowers need pruning to insure maximum quality of bloom, as do roses and other deciduous shrubs. It is necessary to study each individual species to determine how and when this pruning should be done. If the flowers are borne on the new growth, as with *Escallonia* or *Hibiscus,* pruning may be done in the fall in mild climates or spring in the colder ones. This pruning can be quite severe, if large flowers are desired, as the new growth will have ample time to set buds. *Bouvardia,* on the other hand, should be heavily pruned but just following a blooming period.

Plants that set buds on the previous year's growth do not require as much pruning, and if done as above would remove most of the flowers for that year. Such shrubs should have any necessary heading or pruning done during or immediately after blooming. *Daphne odora* and the heaths *(Erica)* are good examples.

Prune to SIMPLIFY and RENEW your shrub. Thin out spent and crowded wood. The shrub will look cleaner and more attractive and the added available food will push dormant buds into growth aided by the increased light and air. This new growth will constantly renew your plant and insure for it a long, healthy life.

Prune back to retain natural shape

Pinch out tip to force side shoots

Diagonal cut above bud to remove old wood

Stub must rot away before wood heals

Cut too close, large wound requires long healing time

Cut heals rapidly when made properly

LS868

Abelia 'Edward Goucher'
GOUCHER ABELIA

A hybrid of the common *A. grandiflora*, similar in habit but more colorful. Has long arching stems always covered with small bronzy-green leaves, and most of the time with fragrant lavender-pink flowers. Grows easily to about 6 feet with a spread of 4 feet. May be partly deciduous in coldest areas. Hardy to zero.

Abutilon speciosum
DWARF ABUTILON

A dwarf strain of Abutilon or Flowering Maple which grows fairly fast to 4 or 5 feet. Rangy and upright in habit unless pinched back. Has light green maple-like leaves and blooms over a long season. Flowers are showy, bell-like and bright orange. Prefers moist soil and half shade. Hardy to about 24 degrees.

LS872

Aucuba japonica maculata
GOLDDUST PLANT

Has big 6- or 7-inch leaves of bright green dusted and flecked with spots of gold. Plant grows irregularly to 6 or 8 feet, with a spread of 4 to 5 feet. Does well in almost any soil and is suitable for deep shade. Bright red berries are borne on female plants when male plant is near by. Hardy to about 15 degrees.

LS874

Arbutus unedo
STRAWBERRY MADRONE

A dense, bushy, evergreen shrub which grows to 10 feet or larger, somewhat less in spread. In fall has pearly-white bell-shaped flowers, followed by clusters of bright red fruit which look like strawberries. Stands heat and drouth. Sun or part shade. Hardy to about 15 degrees.

Aucuba japonica
JAPANESE AUCUBA

Handsome shade-loving plant which grows moderately to 8 or 10 feet, with a spread of 5 or 6 feet. Large shiny leaves provide a tropical effect for planters used outdoors or in. Female plants will bear bright red berries if male plants are near by. Tolerant of almost any soil if it is kept moist. Hardy to about 15 degrees.

151

Beloperone guttata   69
SHRIMP PLANT

A compact little evergreen plant which grows about
2 feet tall and spreads to 15 inches. Coppery-bronze
bracts enclosing little cream-and-purple flowers crown
each plant throughout the year. Excellent for cutting
and arranging. Sun or partial shade. Hardy to about
24 degrees.

Bouvardia 'Coral'

Grows larger than *B*. 'Albatross,' 4 to 5 feet, with a
spread of 2 to 3 feet. The flowers, in big clusters,
are pink or coral in color and differ from those of
'Albatross' in that they have no fragrance. Best in
partial shade, in rich soil and with plenty of moisture.
Hardy to about 22 degrees.

Berberis darwini   LS864
DARWIN BARBERRY

A showy evergreen shrub with a fountain-like growth habit
to 8 feet high and as wide. The small holly-like leaves are
dark green above and light green beneath. Bears clusters of
golden yellow flowers tinged with red in early spring followed by dark blue or purple berries. Hardy to about
5 to 10 degrees.

Bouvardia longiflora 'Albatross'
WHITE BOUVARDIA

Informal little evergreen shrub, 2 to 3 feet tall, slightly
less in spread. The chief attraction is the display of white
tubular flowers with an intense jasmine-like fragrance.
Blooms most of the year but an occasional pruning helps
keep flowers coming. Needs shade in warm, dry areas.
Hardy to about 25 degrees.

Brunfelsia calycina floribunda
YESTERDAY-TODAY-AND-TOMORROW

A fine compact medium shrub (6 feet tall by 5 feet across) heavily foliaged with dark green lustrous leaves. Throughout half the year has intensely fragrant 2-inch flowers which open violet, fade to lavender, and finally to white. Likes part shade, and moisture. Hardy to about 20 degrees.

731

116

Calliandra guildingi
TRINIDAD FLAME BUSH

A graceful open shrub with lacy fern-like foliage. Grows to 6 or 8 feet with about the same spread. During spring and summer each branch bears terminal clusters of fiery flowers with showy bright red stamens. Needs full sun and good drainage. Hardy to about 18 degrees.

Callistemon citrinus
LEMON BOTTLEBRUSH
Syn. *C. lanceolatus*

A narrow-leaved, fast-growing, evergreen shrub or small tree, from 10 to 25 feet in height, with a spread of 6 to 10 feet. Brush-like flowers of brilliant red are borne profusely in spring and again in the fall. Grows easily in full sun. Hardy to about 15 degrees.

LS418

LS869

Ceanothus 'Julia Phelps'
CALIFORNIA LILAC

The ceanothus, native of California, is well adapted to plantings where little care is intended, as on hillsides. It requires good drainage and little moisture when established. *C.* 'Julia Phelps,' a recent hybrid, attains a height and spread of about 6 feet. It has dark green, furrowed foliage. Its inch-long, deep blue flower clusters cover the plant in late spring. Hardy to about 5 degrees above zero.

Calluna vulgaris
SCOTCH HEATHER

This is the native Scotch Heather, a compact little evergreen shrub with each erect branch clothed with close finely-cut foliage. Grows from 1 to 2 feet tall, usually somewhat less in spread. In late summer, August and September, each branch is tipped with a spike of little, rosy-lavender, bell-like flowers. Grows best in cool, moist areas. Hardy to about zero degrees.

LS870

LS871

Ceanothus impressus
SANTA BARBARA CEANOTHUS

One of the most desirable of the ceanothus for garden use. It is handsomely foliaged, densely branched, 3 to 5 feet tall and as much across. In March and April, inch-long heads of deep blue flowers cover the plant. Needs sun, good drainage, low moisture. Hardy to about 10 degrees.

1337

LS873

Cistus purpureus
ORCHID ROCKROSE

A handsome compact plant seldom over 4 feet tall but may be 6 feet across. In spring and early summer displays countless 3-inch blooms of rosy pink with a spot of maroon at the base of each petal. Grows in poor soil, stands heat and drought. Hardy to about 12 degrees.

Correa harrisi
RED AUSTRALIAN FUCHSIA

Valuable, densely foliaged, low-growing, permanent shrub, seldom over 2 feet tall but may spread to 4 feet. From January to April, little bell-shaped flowers of brilliant scarlet hang from each branch. Plant in sun or part shade. Hardy to about 20 degrees.

Convolvulus cneorum
BUSH MORNING GLORY

Grows rapidly and easily to a compact, silvery-foliaged plant, 2 to 3 feet tall with about the same spread. From spring until fall, white trumpet-like blooms of snowy white are displayed continually. Needs full sun for best appearance; almost any well-drained soil. Hardy to about 15 degrees.

LS574

73

Crotalaria agatiflora
CANARYBIRD CROTALARIA

Irregular, fast-growing shrub with soft gray-green foliage. Variable in size but may grow to 10 or 12 feet tall and as much across. The flowers are striking, resembling a host of green-gold canary birds lining each branch. Grows in almost any soil, in full sun. Hardy to about 25 degrees, but recovers quickly if frozen.

LS959

Correa speciosa Syn. *C. pulchella*
WHITE AUSTRALIAN FUCHSIA

Excellent, low-growing evergreen shrub densely clothed with small leaves, deep green above, silvery beneath. Seldom over 2 feet tall but may spread to twice that, or more. All winter, November to April, carries many little, white, bell-like flowers. Other forms of the same species may be red-flowered, pink or even green. Sun or part shade and rather dry soil. Hardy to about 20 degrees.

Cotoneaster lactea
PARNEY'S RED CLUSTERBERRY

One of the most attractive of the cotoneasters; a graceful arching shrub with good-looking soft green foliage. Grows easily to a height of 8 feet, somewhat more in spread. In November and December the plant is loaded with big clusters of bright red berries. Hardy to about 6 degrees.

Daphne odora
WINTER DAPHNE

Neat, slow-growing plant for sunny places. Grows slowly to 4 feet with a spread of 5 feet and has glossy 3-inch leaves. In February and March clusters of intensely fragrant pink flowers appear. Likes ample moisture but good drainage is essential; some morning sun is preferable. Hardy to about 10 degrees.

LS961

LS962

Daphne cneorum
ROSE DAPHNE

Low-growing, evergreen shrub with long, trailing branches crowded with slender dark green leaves. In April and May the branches are tipped with big clusters of little pink flowers. Their fragrance will scent the entire garden. Needs partial shade and demands good drainage. Hardy to about 5 degrees.

LS963

Escallonia organensis
ORGAN ESCALLONIA

1577

A fast-growing, large shrub thickly clothed with bronzy-green 3-inch leaves. Grows to 8 or 10 feet in height and as much in diameter. In early summer displays many broad clusters of rosy-red-to-pink blooms. Full sun on the Pacific Coast, semi-shade inland. Hardy to 15 degrees.

Escallonia rubra
RED ESCALLONIA

Compact shrub with glossy, dark green, 2-inch leaves. Grows in a rather erect manner to about 5 or 6 feet, somewhat less in spread. Has fragrant deep red blooms in clusters most of the year. Particularly good coastal shrub in full sun, but prefers partial shade inland. Hardy to about 15 degrees.

Erica 'John McLaren'

1647

Almost everblooming, and the flower spikes are spectacular — big 6-inch clusters of firecracker-like blooms of clear rose-pink. The plant has needle-like foliage and grows in rather loose fashion to about 2 feet. Best in sun in an acid soil with perfect drainage. Hardy to about 15 degrees.

LS370

Euonymus japonicus aureus
GOLDLEAF EUONYMUS

Fast-growing, rather upright, foliage shrub, which will reach 10 feet or more, but which is usually shaped by trimming. A useful accent plant because of the rich golden color of the foliage. Easily grown but apt to mildew if planted in too much shade. Hardy to about 10 degrees.

Fatsia japonica (in window planter), Tetrapanax papyriferus (far right) 2159

Fatsia japonica (left)
FATSIA
Syn. *Aralia sieboldi*

The giant many-fingered shiny leaves are often 14 inches across, giving the plant a lush tropical look. Grows rapidly from 6 to 10 feet tall, with a spread of 5 to 8 feet. Likes good soil and ample moisture. Grows in sun or shade, but gets leggy in deep shade, pale green in full sun. Hardy to about 15 degrees.

Tetrapanax papyriferus (right)
RICE PAPER PLANT

Slender curving trunks of varying heights up to 12 feet are crowned with clusters of giant, deeply-lobed leaves, downy gray-green above, silvery beneath. The leaves are often 16 inches across on older plants. Tolerates almost any soil, sun or part shade. Hardy to about 22 degrees.

Fremontia mexicana
SAN DIEGO FREMONTIA

A large spreading shrub with broad, grey-green leaves, 15 by 15 feet. In winter and spring the plant glows with masses of 3-inch golden flowers. Needs full sun, good drainage, and very little moisture. Hardy to about 12 degrees.

993

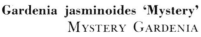

Gardenia jasminoides 'Mystery'
MYSTERY GARDENIA
Syn. *Cape Jasmine*

Grows moderately fast to 4 or 5 feet tall, with the same spread, and has particularly fine, large, shiny foliage. The superb flowers, immaculately white, are intensely fragrant, often 5 to 6 inches across. Needs acid soil, good drainage. Will stand considerable sun. Hardy to about 12 degrees.

LS960

Hibiscus rosa-sinensis 'Kona'
CHINESE HIBISCUS

Showy shrubs with large deep green leaves and a continuous show of huge exotic flowers. Plants vary somewhat by variety but are generally about 8 to 10 feet tall and as much in spread. Flower colors are most commonly white, yellow or red, with many intermediate shades and variations. This hibiscus needs warmth and moisture. Hardy to about 28 degrees.

Hibiscus 'California Gold'

Hibiscus 'Crown of Bohemia'

Hibiscus 'The Bride' 2037

Hibiscus 'Kama Pua' 1646

Hibiscus 'Ross Estey'

LS135

1555

Hypericum kouytchense
KWEICHOW ST. JOHNSWORT

Rounded shrub with pointed light green leaves. Grows 3 to 4 feet tall, with about the same spread, and carries a wealth of golden yellow 2-inch blooms throughout the spring and early summer. Easily grown in almost any soil, in sun or part shade. Hardy to about 10 degrees.

Iberis sempervirens
EVERGREEN CANDYTUFT ▷

Makes a low mound of shiny dark green foliage, spreading to as much as 2 feet but seldom over 1 foot tall. Makes an excellent border or edging. Throughout the spring months, the plant is crowded with tiny snow-white flowers in clusters. Prefers sun or very light shade. Hardy to about 10 degrees.

LS964

Ilex cornuta rotunda
DWARF CHINESE HOLLY

Has the same spiny, thick "square-tipped" lustrous leaves as Chinese Holly, except they are smaller and packed more compactly along each branch. Makes a dense evergreen shrub 3 to 4 feet or more tall, with equivalent spread. Better suited to warm dry areas than *I. aquifolium* or *I. crenata*. Sun or part shade. Hardy to about 5 degrees.

LS965

LS608

Ilex crenata convexa
CONVEXLEAF JAPANESE HOLLY

Compact, bushy, evergreen shrub growing 4 to 6 feet tall and 4 feet across. Somewhat resembles boxwood with its thick mantle of small, rounded, dark green leaves. Stays neat and green the year around. Often used as a hedge. Sun or part shade. Hardy to about 5 degrees.

Ilex cornuta 'Burford'
BURFORD HOLLY

A neat compact plant, slow-growing to 8 or 10 feet, with an equivalent spread. As with most hollies, its development can be speeded by occasional feeding. The leaves are nearly spineless, deep green and glossy. This variety produces large berries freely (often without pollination) and is one of the best hollies for warm dry areas. Sun or part shade. Hardy to about 8 degrees.

1557

LS966

LS942

Kalmia latifolia
MOUNTAIN LAUREL

Grows rather slowly to 6 or 8 feet high and about 6 feet across with a dense round-topped head of 3- to 4-inch pointed leaves. In May and June the branches are tipped with showy clusters of appleblossom-pink blooms. Cultural requirements similar to those of rhododendron. Dislikes heat, low humidity and alkalinity. Hardy to zero degrees or below.

1925

Ligustrum japonicum
WAXLEAF PRIVET

May grow 6 to 10 feet tall, but is generally used to make a dense 4- or 5-foot hedge. Has abundant thick, glossy leaves 3 to 4 inches long. Like other privets, will grow under widely varying conditions of soil and climate. Hardy to about 10 degrees.

LS943

Leucophyllum frutescens
TEXAS SILVERLEAF

Compact, rather slow-growing plant with thick silvery-gray foliage, which grows to about 5 or 6 feet, with a spread of 4 feet. Displays a profusion of little lavender-pink blooms in late summer. Excellent for hot, dry places. Hardy to about 10 degrees.

Lonicera nitida   LS947
BOX HONEYSUCKLE

Small evergreen shrub growing to about 6 feet in height with a spread of 4 feet. May be sheared in same manner as boxwood. Tolerates partial shade. Hardy to about 5 degrees above zero.

Mahonia aquifolium   653
OREGON GRAPE

Rather erect to 4 or 6 feet, but may vary by area. Leaves are large and holly-like, with the new growth a rich bronzy red. Abundant yellow flowers in spring are followed by big blue-purple berries. Can be grown in sun but prefers shade in dry or colder areas. Hardy to zero.

Nandina domestica   LS948
HEAVENLY BAMBOO

A very attractive small shrub with slender, pointed, bamboo-like leaflets. New leaves are bronzy-red turning to bright green. Then the entire plant turns coppery-red during winter. Large bright red berries appear in the fall, but only if two plants are present for cross-pollination. Grows 3 to 4 feet tall and about 3 feet across. Useful as a single specimen or in a hedge. Sun or part shade. Hardy to about 5 degrees.

Melianthus major   LS951
BIGLEAF HONEYBUSH

Giant-toothed gray-green leaves, a foot or more across, make this a striking plant for use as a garden accent. Grows in a rather sprawling manner and looks best if kept 3 to 5 feet tall by pruning. Tolerant of almost any soil, sun or shade. Hardy to about 22 degrees.

LS952

Nerium oleander
OLEANDER

Makes an open shrub 12 feet or more in height, but may be trained as a small tree. Long willowy branches with good-looking foliage are loaded with colorful bloom from May to October. Excellent for hot, dry areas, but also good under average conditions. Hardy to about 15 degrees.

Ochna multiflora
PEARLEAF

Grows irregularly to 4 or 6 feet, the same in spread, and is never without interest. In spring the leaves turn to bronze, then masses of yellow flowers appear in summer, followed by jet-black berries set on bright red cushions. Needs moisture and good drainage. Hardy to about 22 degrees.

1217

Osmanthus delavayi
DELAVAY OSMANTHUS
Syn. *Siphonosmanthus*

Handsome shiny-foliaged shrub with arching branches which grows rather slowly to 6 feet in height, with about the same spread. From March to May, clusters of tiny white flowers will scent the garden with their heavy hyacinth-like fragrance. Prefers semi-shade and acid soil. Hardy to about 20 degrees.

LS953

2033

LS956

Photinia serrulata
Chinese Photinia

Large evergreen shrub, 15 feet or more in height, unless kept smaller by pruning. The big-toothed leaves turn bronzy in spring, and an occasional one bright red during the summer and fall. White flowers in spring are followed by bright red berries. Grows easily in full sun or part shade. Hardy to about 5 degrees.

Pieris japonica
Lily-of-the-Valley Shrub
Syn. *Andromeda*

Evergreen shrub from 6 to 10 feet tall with a spread of about 6 feet. The new growth each spring is bronzy, changing to dark green. Displays weeping clusters of pearly-white blooms in early spring. Slow growing. Needs an acid soil and grows best in a cool, moist climate. Hardy to about 5 degrees.

Pernettya mucronata
Chilean Pernettya

Thickly-branched small shrub which grows from 2 to 3 feet tall. Has small shining dark green leaves all year, some of which turn bronzy or red during winter. Little nodding white flowers in late spring are followed by showy ½-inch berries (usually red) which hang on all winter. Prefers sun and moist but well drained soil. Hardy to about 15 degrees above zero.

LS955

Pieris forresti
CHINESE PIERIS

LS944

Similar to *P. japonica* in habit and cultural requirements, but this grows faster, has larger leaves and larger flowers. The new foliage appearing in spring is a brilliant red in color and very showy. Hardy to about 12 degrees.

LS946

Pyracantha 'Rosedale' ®
FIRETHORN

A horticultural variety, naturally erect in habit (to 15 feet or more), and easily trained in espalier fashion. Abundant little white flowers in late spring are followed by huge clusters of dark red berries in late fall. Hardy to about 12 degrees.

Pyracantha coccinea 'Government Red'
FIRETHORN

LS945

One of the hardiest of Pyracanthas, growing as a rounded bush to 8 to 10 feet, or to 20 feet against a support. Produces clusters of white flowers in late spring and bears an abundance of bright red berries in late fall. Hardy to about 5 degrees above zero.

Pyracantha 'Duvali'
FIRETHORN

1517

A lovely form, vigorous, and one of the heaviest fruit-producers among Firethorns. Leaves are deep, glossy green, the variety especially adaptable for espaliers, for training, hedge-fashion, on fences 2 to 8 feet tall, for trellising, for growing on wires to hide walls and bulkheads, or for culture as trees or standards. Fruits larger than 'Rosedale,' about like 'Graber.'

LS949

2046

Ternstroemia gymnanthera

Valuable for the ever good-looking, large, lustrous foliage — dark green, varying to tones of bronze, gold and maroon. Grows rather slowly from 6 to 10 feet in height and spreading to about the same. Has small clusters of cream-white flowers in late spring. Prefers acid soil, partial shade in warm dry areas. Hardy to about 10 degrees.

Raphiolepis indica rosea
PINK RAPHIOLEPIS Syn. *Indian Hawthorn*

A compact shrub, slow-growing to about 4 feet, with a spread of 5 feet. It has handsome foliage, fragrant pink flowers borne in panicles during spring and summer, followed by clusters of blue-black berries. Likes sun or part shade. Hardy to about 15 degrees.

Skimmia japonica
JAPANESE SKIMMIA

A slow-growing compact plant for shade. May become 4 to 5 feet tall with wider spread or may remain lower. Clusters of tiny, white, scented flowers are borne in April and May to be followed, if both male and female plants are present, by brilliant red holly-like berries up to Christmas time or later. Flowers of the male plants are the larger and more fragrant. Best in a cool moist climate. Hardy to about zero degrees.

LS950

Turraea obtusifolia   LS954
STARBUSH

An excellent, small flowering shrub compactly covered with deep green foliage. Grows about 3 feet tall with about the same spread and is sprinkled with snowy-white jasmine-like blossoms from July to November. Best in partial shade, with perfect drainage. Hardy to about 26 degrees.

Viburnum tinus robustum   1924
LAURESTINUS

Large shrub, 6 to 10 feet, densely clothed with shiny, dark green, 3-inch leaves. Covered in late winter or early spring with rose-scented, pinkish-white flowers in 3-inch clusters. Useful as a hedge or single specimen. This variety is more mildew resistant than the common *V. tinus*. Grows readily under varying conditions and is hardy to about 12 degrees.

Xylosma senticosum
SHINY XYLOSMA

An extremely useful evergreen shrub, not only for its beauty but for its ability to stand heat, drouth, cold and almost any soil. It grows to about 5 feet with the same spread. The arching branches are clothed in shiny bright green foliage. Easily grown and hardy to about 15 degrees.

LS335

AZALEAS

Section 40

AZALEAS

Introduction

MANY GARDENERS seem confused when confronted by a plant, to them obviously an azalea, yet labeled *Rhododendron.* Invariably the question arises, "Just what is the difference between the two?" Botanically speaking, azaleas are a section of that large and varied genus *Rhododendron,* although commercial growers have found it expedient to retain the old name azalea for such well known forms as Kurume, Indica, and Mollis hybrids. Many years ago, *Azalea* was considered to be a distinct genus. At that time azaleas were supposed to differ from rhododendrons by their deciduous foliage and their five stamens, whereas the rhododendrons known to botanists of that period were mostly evergreen and had ten or more stamens. As botanical exploration became more widespread the discoveries of collectors revealed many intermediate forms between the two genera, so that the line of demarcation became fainter and fainter. Expeditions into little-known regions of the Orient and Eastern Asia brought back azaleas with evergreen foliage. Rhododendrons with deciduous foliage were discovered. The number of stamens no longer furnished a clue for positive identification of azaleas, so the botanists decided to combine the two within the one genus *Rhododendron.*

The wilds of Eastern Asia and neighboring areas have been the storehouse from which we have received many of our finest ornamentals. Magnolias, camellias, rhododendrons, and lilies are but a few of the numerous genera which have enriched our gardens. Of all the azalea species now in existence, 42 have their origin in the temperate regions of Eastern Asia from Japan and Northern Korea to Southwestern China and the Philippines. From a horticultural standpoint, the North American continent has also contributed generously to our gardens. The native azaleas of our continent are outstanding in their fragrance and beauty. A total of 16 species occur as wildlings in areas from Labrador to Florida and Eastern Texas. On the west coast, the native Western azalea *(Rhododendron occidentale)* is particularly abundant from Southern Oregon to Southern California. One other, the Pontic azalea *(R. luteum* or *flavum)* is an

RHODODENDRON NUDIFLORUM   RHODODENDRON GANDAVENSE   RHODODENDRON INDICUM   RHODODENDRON MOLLE

Azaleas (Continued)

isolated species which occurs in the Black Sea region.

For garden purposes, azaleas may be divided into two main sections, (1) Deciduous Azaleas or those which lose their leaves in winter, and (2) Evergreen Azaleas or those which retain their leaves for most of the year.

Deciduous Varieties

GHENT HYBRIDS

Hybrids of this group were the first to gain popularity and were developed by P. Mortier of Ghent, Belgium, about 1825. They were derived from four North American species, the swamp honeysuckle (*R. viscosum*), the pinxterbloom (*R. nudiflorum*), the flame azalea (*R. calendulaceum*), and the Oconee azalea (*R. speciosum*). To this quartet was added the Pontic azalea (*R. luteum*) from Eastern Europe. Most of the Ghents are delightfully fragrant and the color range extends from white through shades of yellow to orange, red and various tones of pink. Many of them appear to be hardy to 25 degrees below zero but do not perform too well in areas where summer temperatures are extreme.

MOLLIS HYBRIDS

About 1870 this group was created by combining two oriental species, the eastern Chinese azalea (*R. molle*) and the Japanese Mollis azalea (*R. japonicum*). They differ from the Ghents in that the flowers are slightly larger and they do not have the slender tube which is so characteristic of the latter. The Mollis hybrids do not have the fragrance of the Ghents and are not quite as hardy. The color range is heavy in the oranges and yellows, although there are several varieties which come in rose and pink shades.

EXBURY HYBRIDS

The real advance in the deciduous hybrid groups came in 1850 when Anthony Waterer, Sr., of Knap Hill, England, began to combine selected forms of *R. molle* and *calendulaceum* with the Ghent hybrids. Later he used forms of *R. japonicum, arborescens,* and *occidentale* with the Ghents to create what is now known as the Knaphill hybrids. The late Lionel de Rothschild obtained a selection of the best forms from Knaphill and immediately went to work on an intensive program of re-selection and breeding to create the now famous Exbury deciduous azaleas. His years of patient labor have resulted in a group of azaleas with a wide color range from pure white to soft pastel shades, fiery reds, oranges, and deep yellows. The flowers are immeasurably superior to the Mollis types and have broad petals giving them a squarish look. Their blooming season extends from early May until early July and the flowers are carried in large trusses. In some varieties, their size approaches that of rhododendrons. Most of the Exbury azaleas will form husky shrubs averaging from four to six feet in height and three to four feet wide. Some have withstood temperatures to 25 degrees below zero and most do well in full sun except that the flowers do not retain their fresh look for long if the day is warm. To see them at their best therefore the plants should be given the benefit of some overhead shade in the heat of the day.

Evergreen Varieties

The term evergreen as it applies to azaleas is a relative one since in some of the groups within this section the plants are almost leafless during the winter

Azaleas (Continued)

months and the only foliage is the few leaves clustered around the flower head. This is particularly true of hybrids derived from *R. kaempferi* and also of some of the Glenn Dale hybrids. By contrast, the Belgian Indian azaleas give the appearance of being completely evergreen. The leaves on most evergreen azaleas are dimorphic which means that there are two sets each year, (1) the larger spring leaves which drop during fall and winter and (2) the smaller leaves, leathery in texture, which are formed in summer and remain on the plants through the winter months.

GABLE HYBRIDS

We are indebted to Joseph Gable of Stewartstown, Pennsylvania, for this group. In creating them, Mr. Gable has extended the climatic zone of the evergreen types, so far as winter hardiness is concerned, by combining the Korean azalea *(R. poukhanense)* and the kaempfer azalea *(R. kaempferi)* with Kurume hybrids plus occasional forms of the Belgian Indian azaleas. From the crosses, he obtained plants hardy to zero and below, with flowers from 1½ to 2½ inches wide and in a wide color selection from white through pink shades, orange reds, and purple.

GLENN DALE HYBRIDS

These result from extensive hybridization by B. Y. Morrison and were developed at the Glenn Dale Plant Introduction Station, Maryland. Mr. Morrison's goal was to obtain a race of azaleas with the size and brilliance of the Southern Indian group yet hardy enough to withstand the winters of the mid-Atlantic States. This he has accomplished in the Glenn Dales. Their parentage is quite complex and includes species and hybrids from practically all of the evergreen types in commerce. In the more than 400 named varieties, there may be found dwarf, medium, and tall forms with ultimate heights from 2 to over 6 feet high and including all color shades presently existing in evergreen azaleas, plus interesting and attractive varieties with flecked and variegated flowers. In the Glenn Dales may be found the largest flowers of all the hardier evergreen azaleas, some measuring up to 4½ inches wide.

BELGIAN INDIAN HYBRIDS

As the name implies this group was developed primarily in Belgium although similar work was done in England, Germany and France. The species involved in the crosses include *R. indicum, mucronatum, simsi, phoeniceum* and possibly *scabrum*. It was intended by the originators that they be used as greenhouse or forcing azaleas. However, where weather conditions permit as in Southern California, they make excellent landscape material. They have wonderfully dense foliage and literally cover themselves with large, showy, single, semi-double or double flowers.

SOUTHERN INDIAN HYBRIDS

So-called because these are the varieties generally seen in the famous azalea gardens of the southeastern part of the United States and were selected out of the Belgian Indian azaleas as being suitable for out-of-doors planting. They are considered to be slightly hardier than the Belgian Indian hybrids and like them are used effectively in the landscape in the milder climates of Southern California and the Southeast.

Azaleas (Continued)

KURUME HYBRIDS

The first representatives of this well known group of dwarf evergreen azaleas were introduced to the United States from Japan about 1915. The various named forms now in the trade have been derived from two or three Japanese species including *R. obtusum* and were created by Japanese gardeners over one hundred years ago. They include such popular varieties as 'Hexe,' 'Hinodegiri,' and 'Coral Bells.' The man chiefly responsible for their popularization in this country was E. H. Wilson of the Arnold Arboretum who saw them bloom in Japan in 1914 and subsequently made arrangements for the importation of fifty varieties to the United States. The Kurumes are exceptionally free flowering with a dense, compact habit and a color range which extends from white, through shades of pink, mauve, lavender and red. Most of them are hardy to about 10 degrees above zero.

PERICAT HYBRIDS

Named after Alphonse Pericat of Collingdale, Pennsylvania, they were bred primarily as greenhouse forcing azaleas. These are believed to be the result of crosses between the Belgian Indian and Kurume azaleas and are almost as hardy as the Kurumes. Individually, the flowers are larger than most Kurumes and resemble the Belgian Indians. Sometimes they are grouped with the Belgian Indians in nursery catalogs.

RUTHERFORDIANA HYBRIDS

These were supposedly the result of crosses between *Rhododendron* 'Pink Pearl,' 'Charles Dickens,' 'Mrs. C. S. Sargent,' and the Belgian Indian and Kurume azaleas, although there is no outward evidence of the rhododendron parentage in the Rutherfordiana azaleas. Nevertheless, this group is distinct and very attractive. The plants are compact with good foliage and are best suited as greenhouse forcing plants. The color range is from white, pink, red, to orange-red and purple. Around San Francisco and southwards to Los Angeles, the Rutherfordiana hybrids are used as landscape items. They perform admirably out of doors in regions where winter temperatures do not fall below 20 degrees.

Azaleas In the Landscape

Most azaleas, whether evergreen or deciduous, are at their best when planted in groups or drifts. An ideal situation for them would be among high trees so spaced as to allow the sun and light to penetrate, yet providing intervals of shade to give the plants some respite from the hot sun. Where there are no trees, then the north or east side of the house or of a high fence would be desirable. It is true that many azaleas will thrive in full sun but the flowers will fade quickly should there be a sudden hot spell and, furthermore, the light pastel shades show to better advantage in the cooler light of the woodland.

Deciduous azaleas are more tolerant in their soil requirements than the evergreen ones and, in the main, are considerably hardier. However, because of their deciduous character, they do not give the year around effect in the garden design that is obtained by the evergreen varieties. Conversely, they will stand up in more ex-

Azaleas (Continued)

AN IDEAL SITUATION FOR AZALEAS

NORTH AND EAST SIDE OF HOUSE OR FENCE PROVIDES
PROTECTION FROM SUN AND WIND

posed locations since the bare stems offer little resistance to winter storms. Without exception, the deciduous types are the most spectacular of all spring flowering deciduous shrubs and are breathtaking when seen in mass displays. If it is possible to select by colors, the orange and yellow shades should be kept by themselves and the pinks and softer shades arranged where they will not be overcome by the stronger tones. A drift of deciduous azaleas skirting the edge of a woodland or against the dark green of pines or other conifers makes an impressive arrangement. They combine beautifully with flowering crabs, cherries, and plums, and with the light green of leafing trees, an underplanting of azaleas gives the grouping a light and charming effect. As an underplanted foil for the colorful blossoms, the old-fashioned forget-me-nots may be sown broadcast around and through the planting to provide a carpet of blue, white, and pink. When variation is needed the evergreen Gable and Glenn Dale azaleas may be interspersed with these other types for there are enough varieties in the pink, white and orange tones in both deciduous and evergreen

azaleas so that combinations of the two will complement one another.

The evergreen azaleas are invaluable plants for landscape use. Kurumes and the dwarf forms of Gables and Glenn Dales arranged in groups at the base of camellias and rhododendrons or other bold-leaved evergreens provide a contrast in texture and composition. Or, if the house is small, they may be used by themselves to give an all-year effect as foundation material. On north- or east-facing slopes or on larger rock gardens they are effective either in or out of flower. The taller-growing Glenn Dales are magnificent once they attain their full height of over 6 feet and may be used as background shrubs or for screen plantings in semi-shady gardens. In the milder parts of the country such as may be found along the west coast from San Francisco south or along the southeastern coastal states the large and showy Belgian Indian types make splendid low, evergreen shrubs.

The cultural needs of azaleas are similar to those of rhododendrons and may be referred to under that heading.

LS550

Azalea Knaphill-Exbury Hybrids

The most beautiful of all the deciduous azalea hybrids and described at length in the preface. These were derived from the Knaphill strain and have large trusses of broad-petaled flowers in a wide variety of shades. The earliest of them begin to open in late April and many are still in bloom in mid-June. Their eventual height is about 8 feet but they may be kept lower by pruning back the old flowering stems directly after flowering. They are apparently very hardy.

▽ Azalea Ghent Hybrid

The variety illustrated is one of the Ghent hybrid azaleas which have been discussed in the preface to this section. Named forms are available in shades of pink, orange, yellow and white. They bloom in late May and may be hardy to 25 degrees below zero. Since many of the named varieties are grafted on the yellow-flowered *R. flavum* (*R. luteum* or *Azalea pontica*) a careful watch should be made so that the understock does not grow from the base and crowd off the hybrid.

▽ Azalea Mollis Hybrid

A Mollis azalea planting.

LS957

LS958

LS919

⬇ Rhododendron mucronulatum
KOREAN RHODODENDRON

This species is one of the few deciduous rhododendrons although it is sometimes referred to as an azalea in the trade. It is a native to Korea, China and Japan and becomes an erect shrub about 6 feet tall with clusters of pale rose-purple flowers. Because of its early flowering character (sometimes as early as February in the Pacific Northwest) the plants should be given the protection of high shade to prevent damage to the flowers from early frosts. Otherwise, the plant is hardy to about 10 degrees below zero.

⬆ Azalea Mollis Hybrids

A famous shrub with clustered campanulate blooms about 2½ inches across borne in great profusion in spring, before the leaves have developed. Grows to a height of 5 feet with a similar spread and performs well in sun or light shade. Mature plants usually assume a pleasing informal character. Suitable as single specimens or in groups and appear to good advantage when planted under deciduous flowering trees. Hardy to 5 degrees below zero.

Azalea Mollis Hybrids
A Mollis azalea planting.

LS920

LS303

Rhododendron schlippenbachi
ROYAL AZALEA

Syn. *Azalea schlippenbachi*

This is native to Korea, Manchuria, and Japan and one of the most exquisite species. The plant is dense in habit and slow to grow but eventually attains a height of about 10 feet. In addition to its lovely fragrant soft rose flowers, which appear in early May, the foliage is very attractive and turns to warm hues of yellow and red in the fall. It is hardy to 15 degrees below zero.

LS921

LS922

Rhododendron nudiflorum
PINXTERBLOOM AZALEA

Syn. *Azalea nudiflora*

One of the native eastern North American species which has made an important contribution to the Ghent and Exbury hybrids. It is a deciduous shrub becoming about 6 feet tall and has light pink flowers appearing in May prior to the expanding leaves. It is hardy to 20 degrees below zero and makes a delightful shrub for the woodland garden.

Rhododendron poukhanense
KOREAN AZALEA

Syn. *Azalea poukhanenis*

A deciduous species from Korea which eventually attains a height of from 3 to 5 feet and makes a densely branched shrub, excellent for massed plantings. The fragrant rosy purple flowers are produced in terminal clusters in May and make a charming contrast when planted with pale yellow Ghent or Exbury azaleas. This species is hardy to about 10 degrees below zero.

LS923

Azalea 'Mme. Alfred Sanders'

(Belgian Indian Hybrid) Large, double, red flowers appearing between December and March.

LS930

LS931

Azalea 'Albert-Elizabeth'

(Belgian Indian Hybrid) A well known variety with 3-inch double, variegated red and white flowers. Blooming period from January to April.

Azalea 'Anchorite'

(Glenn Dale Hybrid) An erect shrub eventually 4 feet high and blooming in late April. Free flowering — each flower 2 inches wide.

LS932

LS936

Azalea 'Buccaneer'

(Glenn Dale Hybrid) An upright grower to 5 feet with 2-inch-wide flowers of brilliant orange-red. Blooms in mid-April.

LS937

Azalea 'Chimes'

(Belgian Indian Hybrid) This choice variety with semi-double red flowers, blooms between December and February.

Azalea 'Caroline Gable'

(Gable Hybrid) A lovely deep rose azalea of medium habit, becoming possibly three feet high in ten years, and blooms in early May.

LS406

LS924

LS925

Azalea 'Eri'; 'Eric Schaeme'

(Belgian Indian Hybrid) This is a compact grower, blooming between December and March.

Azalea 'Coral Bells'

(Kurume Hybrid) A dainty low-growing variety with shell pink flowers which are deeper pink in the center. Flowers in early April.

Azalea 'Everest'

(Glenn Dale Hybrid) A spreading shrub to 5 feet in height with 2-inch white flowers which have a chartreuse blotch within the throat. Blooms in mid-May.

LS926

Azalea 'Fielder's White'

(Southern Indian Hybrid) One of the best large-flowered white Indian azaleas. Opens early in the season. Flowering period from February to April.

LS929

Azalea 'Glamour'

(Glenn Dale Hybrid) Upright to spreading habit and attaining a height of about 5 feet. Large 2- to 3-inch flowers appearing in mid-April.

LS928

Azalea 'Gaiety'

(Glenn Dale Hybrid) A free-flowering plant of erect, spreading habit to 5 feet tall. Blooms in early May.

LS927

LS933

Azalea 'Hinode-Giri'

(Kurume Hybrid) A popular variety with profuse bloom. Dense, compact habit and single, brilliant red flowers in April.

Azalea 'Hexe'

(Kurume Hybrid) A very popular variety with dense, deep green foliage and large hose-in-hose crimson-red flowers in late April.

Azalea 'Jean Haerens'

(Belgian Indian Hybrid) Lovely, frilled, double rose-pink flowers. Blooming period between January and April.

LS934

LS935

LS938

Azalea 'Lambertus C. Bobbink'

(Rutherfordiana Hybrid) Semi-double, carmine-rose flowers, 2¼ inches wide, on compact plants. Tender out of doors, except in frost-free locations. Blooms in April.

LS939

Azalea 'Lorna'

(Gable Hybrid) This variety resembles 'Rosebud,' of which it is a sister seedling, but it is taller and has slightly larger flowers.

Azalea 'Orchiphilla'; 'Orchidiflora'

(Belgian Indian Hybrid) An attractive variety with double orchid-pink flowers. Blooming period from January to March.

Azalea 'Miss Cottage Gardens'

(Belgian Indian Hybrid) A beautiful semi-double, dark red variety. Blooming between December and March.

LS940

LS941

Azalea phoeniceum ▷

(Southern Indian Hybrid) A popular variety with large 3½-inch flowers. Blooms from February to April.

LS904

LS903

△ Azalea 'Paul Schaeme'

(Belgian Indian Hybrid) A striking double salmon-pink. Flowering period from December to March.

LS905

Azalea 'Pink Pearl' ▷

(Belgian Indian Hybrid) Large double apple-blossom-pink flowers from January to April.

Azalea 'Pride of Dorking'

(Southern Indian Hybrid) A plant of excellent habit and large carmine-red flowers. Blooms from February to April.

LS906

LS907

LS909

Azalea 'Professor Wolters'

(Belgian Indian Hybrid) Salmon-rose single flowers with a white edge. Flowering period from January to April.

Azalea 'Purple Splendor'

(Gable Hybrid) The large, frilled hose-in-hose flowers are an unusual shade of orchid purple and appear in early May. The plant is inclined to spread and in ten years should be about four feet tall with a comparable width.

Azalea 'Rosebud'

(Gable Hybrid) A charming dwarf variety with dense habit and double, rose-pink flowers. It blooms in late May and makes a first class shrublet for the front of the border.

Azalea 'Rose Queen'

(Rutherfordiana Hybrid) Plants of spreading habit with double, light fuchsia-pink flowers. Hardy only in frost-free localities. Blooms in April.

LS908

LS910

LS911

Azalea 'Southern Charm'

(Southern Indian Hybrid) A robust grower with good foliage. Flowering period from February to April.

LS912

Azalea 'Sweetheart Supreme'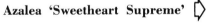

(Pericat Hybrid) A lovely azalea of dense, spreading growth and frilled, deep-rose flowers. In milder climates, where it can be grown out of doors, it blooms in April.

LS913

◁ Azalea 'Treasure'

(Glenn Dale Hybrid) This variety might well replace the older and popular *R. mucronatum (Azalea ledifolia alba)* since it is so much hardier. It is a vigorous grower, eventually 4 or 5 feet high and blooms in late April.

LS914

LS915

Azalea 'Vervaeneana Alba'

(Belgian Indian Hybrid) Large, double, white flowers. Blooming period from January to March.

Azalea 'Vervaeneana Variegated'

(Belgian Indian Hybrid) Flowers large and double. Blooming period from January to March.

Azalea 'Vivid'

(Kurume Hybrid) Although included in the kurumes this is said to have been raised by Charles Sander of Brookline, Mass. A low, densely-branched plant with single red flowers in April.

LS916

CAMELLIAS

Section 50

CAMELLIAS

Introduction

What Are Camellias?

Among plant families, THEACEAE is one of the smallest, and is divided into some sixteen genera of which the most important is *Camellia*. Camellias (in their thirty-odd species) are semi-tropical to temperate plants that are used primarily as ornamental shrubs. Two of the species have become very important as economic plants. *C. sinensis* is grown for its leaves from which tea is made. From the species *C. sasanqua* the seeds are gathered and crushed to extract the oil. From this oil a high quality face cream and hair oil is made. The ornamental species that have become important as flowering shrubs will be taken up later, in the order of their importance or popularity.

The camellia is an ornamental shrub or small tree. It is evergreen, relatively slow growing and reaches maturity in 100 to 125 years. It attains a height of fifteen to thirty feet, depending on the variety. It is used as a shrub rather than a tree because of its slow growth.

Camellias are natives of China, as far south as Cochin, northern Siam, inland China to Yunnan province, coastal China north into Korea. Some species are found on the islands of Japan and Formosa.

Camellias were introduced to the United States, by way of England and France, in 1798. They were first sold as glass house plants in New York, Boston and Philadelphia. A short time later they were widely planted as garden shrubs throughout the southeastern coastal states. The first camellias arrived on the Pacific Coast about 1850. A shipment of plants was sent by boat around the Horn and up the Sacramento river to a nurseryman in Sacramento. Many of these original plants are still growing and, whenever possible, are being moved to the State Capitol grounds.

Camellia Japonica

The forms of this species are the most popular of all camellias and well deserving of this favor. They are broadleaved evergreen plants with beautiful glossy foliage. They are shade loving, but prefer filtered or high shade. They boast a flower form from the single to the complete double, and in between will be found peony form, semi-double, incomplete double, loose peony, rose form, and anemone form. Their color range is from pure white to creamy white, from flesh pink to deep rose, and from scarlet red to black red. Were this not enough variety in color, there are still the variegated flowers. Among these

SINGLE   SEMI-DOUBLE   ROSE FORM   ANEMONE FORM   PEONY FORM   FORMAL DOUBLE

Camellias (*Continued*)

are the pinks blotched white, the reds blotched or marbled white, flowers that are shaded from pink to white, and the whites with candy stripes of pink or red or both.

The flowers range in size from two to six inches across. The keeping quality of the blooms is unsurpassed which makes them ideal for cut flowers or for use as corsages. The fall and winter blooming period sets them apart from most shrubs, and intensifies their desirability as garden or greenhouse shrubs. The varieties bloom at different times. For this reason they are divided into four groups: "E," early bloom (October to December); "EM," early mid-season (December to January); "M," mid-season (February through March); "L," late (April to May). These blooming periods will vary as much as a month earlier for warm areas, and a month later for cooler areas.

There are some twenty-five hundred or more named varieties of *C. japonica*, and it would be impossible to say that any selection of fifty or sixty varieties is the best. Personal likes and dislikes are to be considered, but the following color illustrations are of some of the most popular. For the most part they are older varieties that continue to be popular; others are new but have "proven" themselves.

Camellia Sasanqua, C. Hiemalis, C. Vernalis

C. sasanqua, C. hiemalis, and *C. vernalis* are closely allied species. The foliage and flowers resemble each other and all will stand *full sun* to light shade. The foliage and flowers are smaller than the japonica group, and almost all are fall flowering, starting as early as September. This early fall blooming period is one of the outstanding features of these plants. The flowers range in size from two inches to three inches, and while the bloom shatters after three or four days, they are so floriferous that they present a mass bloom which lasts over a three-month period. They are evergreen and the foliage is glossy dark green about the size of the average rose leaf. Some varieties grow in columns, others are spreading, some globular, others resemble the fir tree in form. This variation in growth habit makes them ideal to use as ground covers, espaliers, for screening, hedge, or almost any job at which one would want to put a plant to work.

The color range is white, many shades of pink, some reds and white with pink or red edging on each petal. Bright golden-yellow stamens enhance their beauty and charm. The versatility of these camellia species makes them highly desirable as garden shrubs, but their potentials are, as yet, to be "discovered" by the average gardener.

Camellia Reticulata

Camellia reticulata has a most startling and beautiful flower. Most varieties have huge blooms that measure up to nine inches. The petals are wavy and are covered with a "glass beading" which gives the flower great depth and beauty. The flower form is from semi-double to double, and the stamens are golden yellow. For the most part the varieties are fast-growing and tall with a rather open habit. They have only about one-third the foliage of the other camellia species, and make only one growth period a season. This should be kept in mind when watering and feeding. Because the plant has less foliage it uses less water than other camellias. Because it has a shorter period of growth, it

Camellias (Continued)

requires less fertilizer. While the shrub seems to stand full sun quite well, the flower does not. For best results give them morning sun or filtered shade.

Camellia Hybrids

Hybridization of camellia species is relatively new to the camellia world, and has not been carried on to any great extent until recently. The hybrid 'J. C. Williams' set off a chain reaction among American hybridists, and at this time much work is being done in this field. Results have been very gratifying and extraordinary plants are being developed.

The J. C. Williams hybrid class shows a mass of blooms over a three-month period or more. The flowers are large, keep well, and are very weather resistant. New shades are being shown but as yet they do not have the full color range of the japonicas. They are, in time, expected to cover a wider range of color than any of the species groups. The foliage is particularly beautiful. The bush is compact and full, with many different growth habits.

To anyone who loves plants this is an exciting world, and the future looks bright and full of wondrous events. Current breeding efforts are centered on bringing the great beauty of camellias to a wider climatic belt with more cold hardiness, also earlier fall blooming.

Landscaping

The great beauty and diversity of the flowers plus their wonderful glossy green foliage, united with good growth habits, make the camellia an ideal plant for landscape uses. All manner of growth habits are to be found which make them one of the most versatile of shrubs. Low squatty varieties are to be found for use in areas where plants must remain low; tall open growers for use as background plants; broad willowy varieties to use as espaliers on fences or trellises; column forms for accent plants; and, in the sasanquas, spreading forms for use as ground covers by use of occasional pruning. Camellias are very well adapted to container culture. They may be grown in pots or tubs, enabling one to move them about as desired. They make a particularly beautiful hedge and one which requires a minimum of pruning. When used in combination with other plants, nothing can or will complement them better.

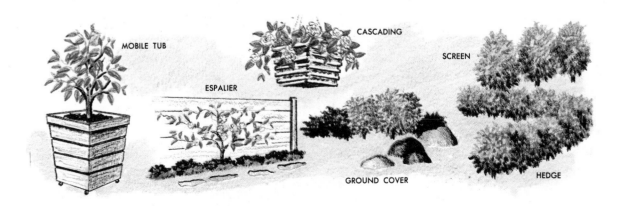

Camellias (*Continued*)

Culture

PREPARATION OF THE SOIL

Basically all camellias require the same culture. They prefer a well-drained soil that is high in humus content and just slightly acid. The acidity of soil for camellias has been exaggerated as they do equally well in soil that is neutral or one that is quite acid with a pH of 5.5. A soil that is more acid than 5.5 will slow the growth.

In preparing the soil for planting in the ground, mix equal portions of sandy loam and peat moss, by volume. If leaf mold is available, it may be used in place of peat moss. The best types of molds come from redwood, pine, eucalyptus (at least one year old), and oak.

For container growing, use a mixture of one part peat moss and one part sand. The sand should be fine, sharp, and uniform.

PLANTING AND STAKING

Dig the planting hole twice as large as the root ball and one and one-half times as deep. Fill the bottom of the hole with the prepared soil and tamp down firmly so that the top of the root ball, when placed in the hole, is one inch ABOVE the soil surface, as there will be some settling. The only way camellias are temperamental is in the depth of the planting. The air requirement of the root is high and, when planted too deep, the roots will smother. The root crown should never be more than two inches below the surface of the soil. Fill in around the sides of the root ball with this same mixture, tamping it down firmly with the feet as you fill, then mound soil three inches high, in the form of a saucer, on the outside rim of the planting hole. Fill this saucer with water.

Some camellias are quite willowy, and when small should be staked. Place the stake close to the main trunk and push into the ground four or five inches. Tie the main trunk loosely to the stake, using as many ties as necessary to bring the plant to an upright position. When the wood matures and hardens, the stake may be removed.

WATERING

Camellias should be moist at all times, but caution should be taken against their being WET at all times. Water well and deeply, but only as often as your own local weather conditions demand. Too much water too often will cut off the air the roots must have. During the flowering period, watering should be watched, as the mature flower is 90% water and a drying out of the plant can cause small blooms, as well as bud drop. Camellias will use large quantities of water during the summer growing periods.

FERTILIZING

Fertilizing or feeding should start with the first signs of growth, even though the plant is still blooming. Plants should be fed only as needed. A commercial food specifically for camellias should be used. Your local nurseryman or garden shop will carry the prepared mixture best suited to your own local conditions. Follow the directions as printed on the package. If the plant is dry, water well the day before feeding; never feed a dry plant.

For plants grown in containers, use one-half the amount as directed, but feed once every month from April to September, with the exception of June. June is a "rest" period, when flower buds are forming. Some reticulatas need feeding in APRIL,

Camellias (Continued)

MAY, AUGUST only. Soak the plant well with water immediately after fertilizing.

CARE AFTER PLANTING

Other than feeding and watering, camellias require very little care. Some insect and pest control is necessary to insure a healthy plant. Scale and mites are the most serious threat as they extract the plant juices and interfere with the normal development of foliage and stem growth.

Mites can cause a premature dropping of foliage, and in severe cases of infestation can cause an almost complete defoliation of the plant. Both mites and scales can be controlled with a spray mixture of 2% summer oil and a 200 to 1 ratio of Malathion mixed in water. Spray once in April or May and again in September. For mites, a follow-up spraying ten days after the initial spraying is recommended to kill the egg hatch.

A program of general spraying every six to eight weeks during the summer months, using nicotine, copper and oil, will insure healthy, pest-free plants. Use spray materials only in the proportions recommended — never stronger.

Very few fungi attack camellias, and the copper in the general spray mixture should control these. *Sclerotinia camelliae*, commonly called petal blight, flower blight or flower rot, is a fungus that attacks camellia flowers. There is no known spray material that will eradicate this disease. The spore is air borne from small black to dark brown toadstools, and when coming in contact with camellia blooms a rotting of the flower occurs. The infected flower falls to the ground, acting as a carrying body, and the following spring when humidity is high and temperatures run 60 degrees or more, the toadstools develop. This life cycle can be broken by keeping all blooms picked up and burned until such time as all flower rotting has stopped.

PROTECTION

C. japonica, C. reticulata and the hybrids need protection from hot mid-day sun. For the flower's sake, the whites and pale pinks will need more shade than the deeper colors. Shade is a very relative term; in climates where humidity is high, camellias can stand more sun than in climates that are hot and dry. *C. sasanqua, C. vernalis*

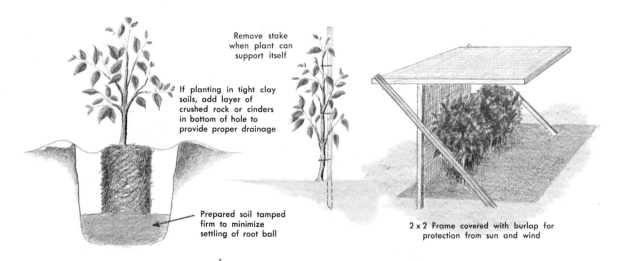

If planting in tight clay soils, add layer of crushed rock or cinders in bottom of hole to provide proper drainage

Prepared soil tamped firm to minimize settling of root ball

Remove stake when plant can support itself

2 x 2 Frame covered with burlap for protection from sun and wind

Camellias *(Continued)*

and *C. hiemalis* are able to stand full sun even in hot dry climates, but do equally well in light shade.

A continuous draft is death to camellias, and a location such as a breezeway or tunneled area should be avoided.

Camellias should be protected from strong winds for the sake of the flowers. As to protection from cold, *C. sasanqua, C. vernalis* and *C. hiemalis* will stand temperatures of 10 degrees above zero to 5 degrees below zero with no injury. The japonicas will stand temperatures to 5 degrees above zero but the complete double flower types will have buds frozen and destroyed at this temperature.

C. reticulata is recommended for very mild areas or glass house culture only. The hybrids, because they are hybrids, will vary from variety to variety as to the cold each

will stand. Some of them have gone through temperatures of zero with little ill effect.

PRUNING

Prune young plants for shape only. Just prior to the growth period is the best time. Do not prune back more than one-third of the plant. Large, old plants need a heavy pruning about every other year. This will promote strong new branches that will support a better quality flower. All dead wood should be removed each year. Pruning for a desired shape is easily accomplished with camellias, but letting your nurseryman help you select a variety best adapted to the desired shape will make the job more easy.

The 'Chandleri' varieties should not have the main stem or trunk cut until they reach the desired height as they have a very difficult time developing a new leader.

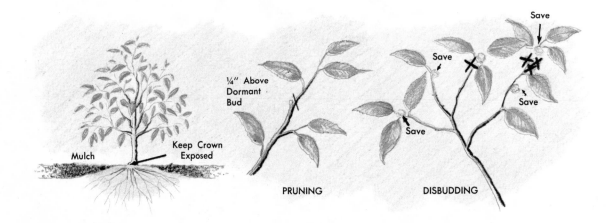

Mulch · Keep Crown Exposed · ¼" Above Dormant Bud · PRUNING · Save · Save · Save · Save · DISBUDDING

LS105

Camellia japonica 'Adolphe Audusson Variegated'

Variegated strain of 'Audusson Red.' Another strain is 'Audusson Special' which is predominately white, streaked red. Growth habits and foliage are the same for all three.

LS773

Camellia japonica 'Adolphe Audusson'
(Audrey Hopfer; Adolphe)

Very large flower that blooms mid-season. Form of bloom varies slightly under different climatic conditions; semi-double to incomplete double. The bush is compact, upright, with dark green, glossy foliage.

Camellia japonica 'Bella Romana'

Bloom is medium large, rose form, mid-season. Growth habit is bushy and vigorous. Foliage, dark green.

Camellia japonica 'Alba Plena'

Very popular early blooming formal, or complete double. Of broad, bushy and upright habit with light green foliage. Blooms profusely over a four to five month period.

LS778

LS777

2505

Camellia japonica 'Bernice Boddy'
(Pat. No. 605)

Vigorous upright grower that carries many small blooms. One of the hardiest.

LS310

Camellia japonica 'Blood of China'
(Victor Emmanuel)

Late bloomer that comes in with a "splash." Strong bushy growth, dark green foliage. Flowers are large.

Camellia japonica 'California'
(Durfee Road)

Makes a handsome bush and has very dark green, thick foliage that stands more than average sun. Blooms mid-season with large flowers and grows stiff, upright.

Camellia japonica 'Carolyn Tuttle'

Medium large peony form. Upright growth habit that stays compact. Foliage is large, dark green. Mid-season to late bloomer.

LS468

2278

2438

Camellia japonica 'Cinderella'
(Pat. No. 1281)

All-America Camellia for 1955-56 season. A sport of 'Waka-noura.' A very large, irregular semi-double, fimbriated and wrinkled on the edges of the petals. Much better performer than its sister sport 'Fred Saunders' which is solid red. Flowers open more freely and frost does not burn the edges of the petals, while in the bud stage, as 'Fred Saunders' does. Late bloomer and the bush is slow in growth and very compact.

Camellia japonica 'C. M. Wilson'
(Grace Burkhard)

Sport of 'Francine' and a "newer" member of the Chandleri group. Has all the good qualities of the Chandleri "family" plus a particularly fine shade of pink.

LS774

Camellia japonica 'C. M. Hovey'
(Colonel Firey; William S. Hastie; Duc de Devonshire; Solaris)

Very large formal, mid-season bloomer. Growth is strong, upright and rather open. Foliage is very dark green.

Camellia japonica 'Covina'

Small flowers but lots of them. Slow, bushy growth with medium small dark green foliage. The only japonica that will stand California's full sun. Makes a fine hedge.

LS103

LS776

Camellia japonica 'Debutante'
(Sara C. Hastie)

Lovely full peony that blooms early to mid-season. Medium large. Growth is very fast and upright with light green foliage. Needs to be pruned for shaping while young.

Camellia japonica 'Daikagura'

Most dependable early variety, blooms from October to March. Large, loose peony form, and grows slow and bushy. Also solid red form is available.

LS287

2415

LS775

Camellia japonica 'Doctor Tinsley'

Blooms in mid-season to late. Growth habit is strong, upright and the foliage is medium dark green. One of the finer new introductions.

LS101

Camellia japonica 'Donckelari'

Very slow growth, and habit is bushy, upright, globular. Blooms mid-season with many large flowers. Foliage is small, glossy, dark green.

LS469

1644

◁ Camellia japonica 'Eleanor Haygood'

Late blooming formal to incomplete double. Light green foliage and bush is compact, upright, medium slow.

◁ Camellia japonica 'Elena Nobile'
(Napa Red)

Grows as a column, but bushy, with dark foliage. The flower is small to medium large and of good color.

◁ Camellia japonica 'Elegans (Chandler)'
(Chandleri Elegans Pink; Francine)

The original of the 'Chandleri' family and the "yard stick" for measuring the good merits of other varieties.

LS284

LS108

Camellia japonica 'Elegans (Chandler) Variegated'
(Chandleri Elegans; Pride of the Emperor's Garden)

Very large anemone form that blooms early mid-season to late. Spreading and slightly pendulous growth habit, large dark green foliage.

Camellia japonica 'Emperor of Russia'
(Stevens Plant)

A mid-season multi-centered flower. Growth is strong, upright and bushy. Foliage is very dark green and glossy and of good size.

LS811

Camellia japonica 'Finlandia'
(Dearest; Nellie White)

The form of this medium large flower puts it "above the average." Bush is compact, upright with dark foliage. Blooms mid-season.

LS288

2132

LS812

Camellia japonica 'Finlandia Variegated'
(Margaret Jack; Aurora Borealis; Speckles)

Foliage, growth habit, etc., are the same as the white form. The light red markings of the bloom will vary with each flower.

Camellia japonica 'Flame'

Mass blooming semi-double with unusually good color of flame red. Mid-season flowering and the growth is stiff, upright but bushy. Dark foliage.

Camellia japonica 'Frizzle White'
(Susan Carter)

Very large, variable flower. Mid-season. Growth is upright and open foliage is large deep green.

LS815

Camellia japonica 'Gigantea'
(Emperor Wilhelm; Magnolia King; Mary Bell Glennan; Fanny Davenport)

Strong, upright, open growth habit with unusually large foliage that is very glossy and dark green. Flower is very large, blooms mid-season, and varies from anemone to peony form.

LS319

LS267

Camellia japonica 'General Dwight Eisenhower'

Slow, bushy and compact growth habit with very deep green foliage. Blooms mid-season, profusely. Also a Variegated form.

LS309

Camellia japonica 'General George Patton'
(Pink Purity)

Large rose-form double, blooms mid-season to late. Strong upright growth, medium green foliage.

LS817

Camellia japonica 'Grandiflora Rosea'
(Louise Maclay; Tea Garden 113) ▷

Vigorous, spreading, compact growing habit with large, dark green foliage. Very large flowers appear from early to mid-season.

◁ **Camellia japonica 'Glen 40'**
(Coquetti)

Superb large formal to rose-form double that blooms heavily, from mid-season to late. Bush is slow, compact, upright in growth with deep green foliage.

LS470

◁ **Camellia japonica 'Guilio Nuccio'**

Very large semi-double to irregular double and a mid-season bloomer. Bush is vigorous, upright with large dark green foliage.

LS818

Camellia japonica 'Herme'
(Hikari-Genji; Jordan's Pride; Souv. de Henri Guichard) ▷

Very slightly fragrant is this medium large semi-double that blooms in mid-season. Grows upright and a little open in habit.

LS178

Camellia japonica 'High Hat'

Sport of 'Daikagura' and has the early blooming habit and spreading growth of the parent. Needs more shade than the parent, for best blooms.

LS286

Camellia japonica 'Joshua E. Youtz'
(White Daikagura)

Very early blooming and flowers are very large. Growth is slow, upright and bushy and foliage is deep green.

2053

2423

Camellia japonica 'Kramer's Supreme'
(Pat. No. 1583)

Very large peony-form with petaloids and petals mixed. Medium fast growth that is compact and upright. Blooms mid-season.

LS100

Camellia japonica 'Kumasaka'
(Lady Marion; Jeanne Kerr; Maiden; Sherbrooke)

Medium slow growth but upright and very compact. Foliage is long and narrow, dark green. Blooms mid-season to late and is an exceptionally heavy bloomer. Flower is medium large to large.

Camellia japonica 'Lady Kay'

LS467

Very floriferous, blooms early to late. Flowers are variable from full peony-form to semi-double, as influenced by climatic conditions. Growth is slow, very compact and upright.

Camellia japonica 'Lallarook'
(Laurel Leaf; L 'Avenir)

LS813

Strong, bushy, upright growth habit with long, narrow leaf. Large flowers appear freely on the bush from mid-season to late.

Camellia japonica 'Magnoliaeflora'
(Rose of Dawn; Hagoromo; Cho-No-Hagasane)

LS814

Medium sized flowers are borne in profusion on a rather slow-growing shrub that is compact and upright. Flowers need more than average shade for lasting quality.

Camellia japonica 'Margarete Hertrich'

Medium large, numerous-petaled complete double. Bush is vigorous, compact, spreading. Flowers mid-season to late.

LS472

Camellia japonica 'Mathotiana'

(Julia Drayton; Mathotiana Rubra; Purple Dawn; Purple Emperor; Purple Prince; William S. Hastie)

Very large blooms that are climatically variable from semi-double to complete double. Rapid growth that is spreading but upright with extra large dark green foliage. Blooms mid-season.

Camellia japonica 'Mathotiana Rosea'

(Pink Beauty; Laura Polka; Warwick)

Late-blooming formal that is very large and needs protection from winds. The plant grows rapidly, becoming upright and rather open. Large light green foliage.

62

2123

LS483

LS816

Camellia japonica 'Monjisu'

(California Donckelari Var.)

Mass bloomer that puts on its own show in mid-season. Rose-form double. Bush is medium slow and very compact. The foliage is deep green and many-leaved.

Camellia japonica 'Mrs. Charles Cobb'

One of the few "black" red Camellias. Large peony-form that blooms early to early mid-season, usually mid-season. Bush is vigorous, upright and compact, and foliage is large and very deep green.

LS724

◁ **Camellia japonica 'Mrs. Nellie Eastman'**

Peony- to rose-form, mid-season flowering. Medium large. Bush is upright and compact, of slower-than-average growth.

LS104

Camellia japonica 'Mrs. Tingley' ▷

Medium sized formal with somewhat slow and compact growth that is a little willowy.

Camellia japonica 'Pax' ▷
(Snow Doll; Yuki-Daruma; White Laurel Leaf)

Large, formal double that blooms late. Bush is upright, compact, medium fast.

LS471

◁ **Camellia japonica 'Nagasaki'**
(Lady Audrey Buller; Mikenjaku; Candida Elegantissima; Tennin-Kwan; S. Peter Nyce)

Vigorous, upright but compact grower that blooms early to mid-season with very large incomplete double flowers. White marbling varies with several strains. Foliage is handsome.

Camellia japonica 'Pink Ball'

Free-flowering peony-form that blooms early to early-mid-season. Bush is vigorous, upright, compact. Medium sized flower.

LS795

Camellia japonica 'Pink Perfection'
(Frau Minna Seidel; Goishi; Usu-Otome; Lacy Pink)

Profuse bloomer but is temperamental because of dropping buds in the cooler coastal areas. Growth is vigorous, compact and upright. Blooms early to late.

1640

LS289

Camellia Japonica 'Princess Baciocchi'

Medium large semi-double to incomplete double that blooms mid-season to late. Bush is broad and globular, with very dark green, glossy foliage.

2424

Camellia japonica 'Prince Eugene Napoleon'
(Pope Pius IX; Imbricata Rubra Plena; Lardiner's Red; Venus De Medicis)

Medium large, many-petaled formal that blooms mid-season. Shrub is spreading but compact and foliage is medium green.

Camellia japonica 'Professor Charles S. Sargent'

Medium sized peony-form to anemone form that blooms mid-season to late mid-season. Plant grows upright and bushy, with very dark foliage.

LS808

Camellia japonica 'Purity'

(Neige d'Oree; Shiragiku; Harriet I. Laub; Refinement; Renjo-No-Tama)

Medium rose-form to complete double that blooms late. Bush is upright, compact, strong. Medium green foliage.

LS797

⇨ Camellia japonica 'Reg Ragland'

A newer variety that is here to stay. Very large blooms are borne on a very compact but upright shrub. Flowers from early to late. The parent of this variety, 'J. J. Fringle Smith,' has magnolia-type flowers borne on a low, spreading shrub that is unusual and very beautiful.

LS809

Camellia japonica 'R. L. Wheeler'

(Patent No. 1137)

Very large semi-double to anemone form. Bush is compact and upright with large, dark green foliage.

LS798

LS801

Camellia japonica 'Sweetheart' ▷
(Patent pending)

All-America Camellia for 1959. Large formal double that blooms mid-season to late. Bush is upright and compact with medium green foliage.

◁ **Camellia japonica 'Shiro Chan'**

The white form of the 'Chandleri' family, derived from 'C. M. Wilson.' Flower is pure white, to white with faint pink flush showing at the base of the guard petal.

LS802

◁ **Camellia japonica 'Te Deum'**
(Dr. Shepherd; Firegold; Moragne; Pasha of Persia; Shah of Persia)

Very large formal to anemone-form, late-blooming variety of unusual color. Plant is fast growing, upright but quite open.

LS803

Camellia japonica 'Ville De Nantes' ▷

Slow-growing, upright and compact plant that blooms mid-season to late. Flowers are semi-double, large and usually have fimbriated petals on the Pacific Coast, but tend to lose the fimbriation in the south Atlantic States.

LS292

Camellia hybrid 'Donation'

Comes to us from England and grows upright and bushy, developing fairly rapidly. Blooms with a splash over a two-month period but some blooms over a four-month period. Mid-season to late. Medium sized foliage that resembles the form of *C. reticulata*.

Camellia vernalis 'Hiryu'
(Flying Dragon; Hiryo; Red Bird)

Small rose-form double flowers that open in the early fall. Rather open, willowy growth which responds to pruning. Resembles the *C. sasanqua* but does not take the hot sun as well; best in light noonday shade.

LS806

LS804

LS807

Camellia hiemalis 'Shishi-Gashira'
(Lion's Head; Beni-Kan-Tsubaki)   LS805

A winter bloomer and a spreading, slow grower which must be staked if height is desired. Makes shrub for low massing, or tub specimen.

Camellia hiemalis 'Showa-No-Sakae'
(Glory; Glory of Showa)

Fast-growing, compact, low-growing shrub but can be staked to an upright habit. A most versatile shrub that can be used as a tub plant, specimen, espalier or hedge, or as ground cover by heavy and continuous pruning.

Camellia reticulata 'Crimson Robe'

2355

(Great Peach Bloom; Large Crimson)

Extra large semi-double with crepe-textured petals. Growth is vigorous and spreading.

Camellia reticulata 'Chang's Temple'

LS796

Very large irregular peony that blooms in mid-season. Vigorous compact growth.

Camellia reticulata 'Buddha'

(Patent No. 1215)

All-America Camellia for 1958 season. Very large irregular semi-double. Grows tall, upright and a little open. Very heavy bloomer in mid-season.

Camellia reticulata 'Butterfly Wings'

(Great Butterfly Wings; Thick Leaf Butterfly; Thick Leaf Butterfly Wings)

Very large irregular to fluted semi-double, rose-pink fading to a blush-pink. Wavy petals resemble butterfly wings in shape. Plant is a rapid, upright grower, slightly open in habit but responds to pruning if one wishes a more compact bush. Long blooming period as compared to other varieties of *C. reticulata*.

2473

2425

LS799

▽ Camellia sasanqua 'Jean May'

Vigorous, upright growth. Starts to bloom in October. A good specimen shrub which can also be trained as an espalier.

△ Camellia sasanqua 'Apple Blossom'

Vigorous, upright growth that remains compact. Starts blooming in September. Good as a hedge or specimen plant.

LS810

Camellia sasanqua 'Ko-Gyoku' ▷
(Ruby; Little Gem; Kogyoku)

Grows as a compact column. Best used as espalier or accent plant. Flower lasts longer with a little shade but will also stand full sun.

LS800

RHODODENDRONS

Section 60

RHODODENDRONS

Introduction

THE GENUS RHODODENDRON is a member of the Heath family and contains over 800 species which occur mainly in the temperate regions of the northern hemisphere. In the United States there are twenty-three native species, including Azaleas which are classified as Rhododendrons by the botanists. So far as hybrid rhododendrons are concerned, the most important native species in this country are the great laurel *(R. maximum),* found growing wild in New England and extending southwards through the Appalachians to northern Georgia, and the mountain rose bay *(R. catawbiense)* which is found on the higher elevations of the Allegheny and Appalachian Mountains. These two species are not as beautiful as our present-day hybrids, but their influence on the cultivated varieties has been and will continue to be most extensive. Perhaps their chief contribution is their ability to withstand below-zero temperatures, a factor of great importance to our present day hybridists.

It is interesting to note that the first rhododendron species to be introduced to cultivation in England was *R. maximum,* whose flowering was recorded in 1756. *R. ponticum* arrived in England from Asia Minor in 1763, *R. caucasicum* in 1803 and *R. catawbiense* in 1809. The famous scarlet tree species, *R. arboreum,* was introduced from China in 1802 and once seen in flower was quickly combined with the earlier arrivals to give us a combination from which many of our finest hybrids have been derived. About the middle of the nineteenth century botanical explorations in the Indian Himalayas, Tibet and Western China became more frequent and a vast array of new species began to find their way into the gardens of Europe to be cultivated and constantly improved so that today we are beginning to reap a harvest of beauty from a genus whose variations in color, floral shape, and leaf pattern are unexcelled.

Landscape Uses

With the increase in number and variety of rhododendron hybrids the gardener has acquired a great deal more latitude in his choice of suitable locations for their display. To facilitate the proper selection of types a fair estimate of the plant's ability to withstand winter temperatures is included under the descriptive captions with each illustration and also an indication of the height of the plant in ten years is stated. The low-growing varieties such as 'May Day,' 'Fabia,' 'Blue Tit,' 'Unique' and 'Bowbells' are supplying a long-needed change of material for foundation plantings and landscape architects are using them to good advantage in north or east aspects or in other situations where shade conditions warrant their use. Such low, compact types are particularly valuable for garden placement around low, one-storied homes and may be used with good effect at the entrance or grouped under windows. Informal hedges of 'Blue Tit' make attractive boundaries between garden areas and are useful as accent plants on larger rock gardens, provided they are not planted on a south-facing slope in full

Rhododendrons *(Continued)*

sun. The medium growing varieties as, 'Blue Peter,' 'Jean Marie de Montagu,' 'Mrs. Furnival,' etc., make wonderful specimen plants for entrance ways or in the shrub border where the handsome foliage gives a splendid contrast to lower plantings of small-leaved shrubs and summer flowering annuals. In larger gardens where they can be planted en masse rhododendrons are unequalled for the brilliance of their display in spring and, because of their bold evergreen foliage, impart a permanent effect to the garden design. The lavender, blue, mauve and soft pastel shades are most striking when planted in shade and such varieties as 'Mrs. Chas. Pearson,' 'Mrs. E. C. Stirling' and 'A. Bedford' make a charming picture in the cool light of the woodland garden. There are varieties suited to the smallest city garden or the largest country estate. The color range is almost complete and includes creams, yellows, lavenders, blues, pinks in every shade, reds, crimsons, scarlets, and many intermediate blends.

Culture

PREPARATION OF SOIL

The accounts of botanical travelers tell us that in the alpine meadows of Yunnan some species are found along the margins of boggy meadows, while others are found thriving on thin layers of humus overlying rocky strata, irrigated by the melting snows from above. These variations in soil types provide a clue to the requirements of rhododendrons in cultivation. An abundance of moisture at the roots is essential, particularly during spring when the plants are putting out their greatest growth. However, sharp drainage along with moisture is also essen-

tial, for without air the roots will not function properly and the plants will show signs of distress. Their roots are exceedingly fine and hair-like. They are confined to the upper 9 to 12 inches of soil and because of their fineness are unable to penetrate a heavy clay or to survive in a wet soggy medium. It has been demonstrated by soil scientists that rhododendrons succeed best in an acid medium, preferably with a pH reading of between 5 and 6. This may not mean too much to the home gardener whose concern is chiefly with the physical structure rather than the chemistry of the soil. If roses, pansies, and lilies are thriving, and if the temperatures are not extreme or humidity too low, then rhododendrons may be grown with reasonable success. A good soil should contain an abundance of humus. If it runs together when wet, or packs and becomes cracked when dry, then add generous amounts of peat moss or decaying leaves. In the case of sticky clay soils, it would be wise to build a bed of loose humus material on top of the clay and then plant the rhododendrons, rather than attempt to make the original soil friable by digging in the humus. If this is not feasible, then apply a dressing of gypsum (calcium sulphate) at the rate of four pounds per 100 square feet and cultivate it in. This will flocculate the clay and make the soil easier to work. Bulky material in the form of peat, leaf mold or decayed pine needles may be incorporated to provide the porosity which is so essential. In sandy soils, the addition of humus is also a necessity, not so much to keep it open but to help retain moisture during the dry months. The cardinal points to remember in the preparation of soil for

Rhododendrons (Continued)

rhododendrons are : (1) lots of humus, (2) sharp drainage, and (3) plenty of moisture.

PLANTING

As was mentioned in the previous paragraph, the roots of rhododendrons are confined to the top 9 to 12 inches of the soil. It therefore follows that they should be planted so that the top of the root ball, as it arrives from the nursery, is not more than one inch beneath the surface. If the roots are placed too deep, it is not long before the foliage turns a sickly yellowish green, growth is short, numerous small flower trusses are produced and the plant ultimately dies from insufficient aeration. If the bed has been prepared with the components recommended in the previous paragraph, then further addition of humus is unnecessary.

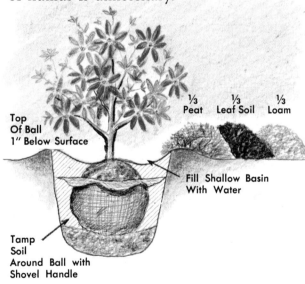

Top Of Ball 1″ Below Surface

⅓ Peat ⅓ Leaf Soil ⅓ Loam

Fill Shallow Basin With Water

Tamp Soil Around Ball with Shovel Handle

Should the planting area be too large to treat as a unit, then dig a hole several inches in excess of the ball's depth and width, break up the bottom of the hole to insure good drainage, then fill around the roots with equal parts of peat moss, leaf mold, and sandy loam. Firm this mixture with a shovel handle, leaving a shallow basin around the plant which should be filled several times with water to settle the root ball. In the Pacific Coast areas west of the Cascades, planting may be carried out from August until May but preferably in the early fall so that the plants have time to become established before new growth is made in the spring. This is particularly important in the warmer areas of coastal California since hot days are often frequent in April and May. Along the eastern seaboard, rhododendrons should be in the ground not later than the middle of October. Failing this, then planting had better wait until spring when all danger from freezing weather has passed.

WATERING, MULCHING

When rhododendrons are purchased from the nursery, the root ball usually contains a high percentage of peat moss. This is especially true in the case of plants in smaller grades. Once peat moss is allowed to become dry, it takes some time for water to penetrate thoroughly into the root ball. To avoid possible injury to the plant due to dry roots, immerse each ball in a tub of water preparatory to planting and then water thoroughly after the plant is in place. On steep slopes, or in the case of large specimens, it is sometimes necessary to resort to sub-irrigation in order that the water may reach the entire root area, in which case the use of a water spike is recommended. This is an attachment which fits on the hose and is pushed into the root area and the water is forced into the ground through holes in the tubular attachment. The canvas hose types of sprinklers, called "soil soakers," are excellent for

Rhododendrons (Continued)

watering and do a thorough job without eroding the soil or dissipating the moisture into the atmosphere. Most rhododendrons are native to regions where the humidity is relatively high so that during the warm summer days, overhead sprinkling night and morning is appreciated, and assists materially in the reduction of insect populations.

4" Mulch of Loose Material

A protective mulch over the roots of rhododendrons is an important part of their culture. Peat moss, decaying pine needles, dried fern leaves, spent hops, tan bark, and sawdust are among the most common mulches which have been used successfully. A mulch should be applied immediately after planting and it should be renewed each year or as it decays to where it is no longer evident on the surface. A mulch protects the root system from the sun's rays and drying winds, keeps the soil temperature warmer in winter and cooler in summer, conserves moisture in dry weather and ultimately becomes a source of food available to the surface feeding roots. Such material as tan bark or sawdust will not break down as rapidly as pine needles or leaf mold. Therefore, they would not be renewed as frequently as the "softer" materials.

FERTILIZING

Rhododendrons are not heavy feeders and a little care in the preparation of the planting site in the beginning will yield big dividends. Leaf mold, peat moss, and other humic materials are usually sufficient and the addition of fertilizers is not really necessary. As a matter of fact, several of the hybrids are quite sensitive to the presence of quickly soluble nitrogenous fertilizers and show their resentment in their deformed and twisted leaves and, in some instances, the foliage takes on a burned appearance around the margins of the leaves. This is particularly true in many of those of *R. griersonianum* parentage.

It is advisable, therefore, to create a reservoir of slowly available plant food in the form of humus material rather than apply the quicker-acting chemical salts in the hope of obtaining quick growth. An exception to this rule is in regard to the use of sawdust as a soil amendment or mulch. In areas close to lumbering industry, it is cheaper than peat moss, serves the same purpose as a mulch, and is an excellent physical conditioner for either a heavy or light soil. In time it becomes a source of plant food, but the period of decomposition is a lengthy one unless quick-acting nitrogenous fertilizers are added. For every one hundred square feet of sawdust one inch thick, apply two pounds of sulphate of ammonia, either dry or in solution.

Whatever method is used, it is good insurance to water the plants thoroughly after applying the fertilizer so that there is no likelihood of a burn. The sulphate of ammonia may be applied in the spring

Rhododendrons (Continued)

and again in three applications at six week intervals. On older specimens which have been in place for some years, a top dressing of well decayed barnyard manure is beneficial if applied in fall as a mulch and allowed to be washed in by winter rains and snow. There are several brand name acid fertilizers on the market, usually with a cottonseed meal base which are slow acting and safe to use when manufacturer's directions are followed.

Care After Planting

Most of the difficulties encountered by gardeners in pursuit of their hobby may be attributed to improper cultural practices. Perhaps the most common error on the part of the grower is planting rhododendrons too deep, as may be indicated by short annual growths, increasingly smaller trusses and leaves, and finally the demise of the plant.

Yellowing of the foliage may be caused by several conditions. If the leaf turns yellow while the veins remain green, it would indicate that the soil is too alkaline and the plant is suffering from iron chlorosis. Such a condition may be temporarily corrected by applying acid fertilizers or by treating the soil or foliage with one of the chelated iron compounds. But it is doubtful that either of these would be of much permanence, so that the only worthwhile solution is to dig up the plant and replant in a humus material such as was recommended in the paragraph on soils.

Overall yellowing of the foliage may be caused by an improperly drained soil and a consequent reduction of oxygen at the root zone. The degree of yellowing differs from that caused by an alkaline soil in that the leaf is yellow all over, including the veins. The remedy is obvious, namely, to provide better drainage either by tiling or by removing the plant to a more suitable location. Too much light will also cause a yellowing of the foliage, particularly on the larger leaved hybrids as the *R. loderi,* 'Dr. Stocker,' etc.

The failure of plants to form flower buds is sometimes encountered. In the case of *R. loderi,* 'Gill's Crimson,' 'Faggetter's Favorite,' 'Beauty of Littleworth,' etc., buds are not produced until the plants are several years old. This is a normal situation and due to inherited characters. Too much overhead shade may cause little flowering wood to be formed and in its place promote a leggy, thin growth. Some hybrids may give an abundance of flowers one year and the next year form only vegetative buds. This condition can be overcome by partially disbudding in the early spring, allowing one flower bud to remain per square foot of leaf area. This will insure an even show of flowers from one year to the next.

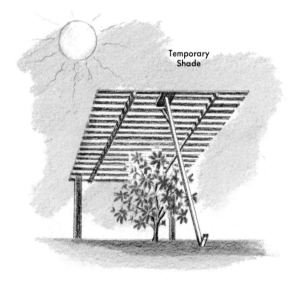

Temporary Shade

Rhododendrons (Continued)

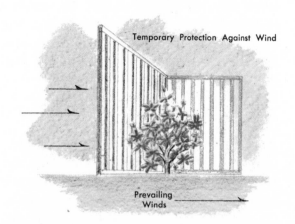

Temporary Protection Against Wind

Prevailing Winds

PROTECTION

Around the home or in the garden where the quality of the bloom is of utmost importance, it is recommended that the plants receive a few hours respite from direct sunlight during the heat of the day.

If the plants are being used as a foundation planting, then the north or east side of the house is to be preferred unless there are trees on the south and west sides to protect them. The ideal location is where the plants receive the benefit of shade from high trees without being directly underneath the branches. It must be borne in mind that it is just as important to protect the plants from strong winds as it is to provide shade, and a belt of high shrubs, or a high fence to the windward side, will prevent a great deal of damage to the foliage as well as the blossoms. Dense overhead shade is detrimental to their welfare and induces the plants to become drawn and leggy with a consequent reduction in vigor and in number of flower buds. Where rhododendrons are planted in woodland, a periodic thinning out of overhead branches is necessary to admit sunlight. In a new garden where shade is insufficient or where the trees have not attained the size to throw much shade, then temporary lath shades will make a splendid substitute until the trees become more mature. When selecting a planting site, avoid hollows or slopes which lead into a hollow where cold air is likely to settle. Such a location can prove to be disastrous during winter and early spring. If possible, choose a long gentle slope where there is a free escape for cold air as well as excess water.

In climates known to be severe, rhododendrons will need protection during winter to ward off extremes in temperatures. This may be accomplished by building a wooden frame structure covered with heavy burlap sacking. Within the frame the plant should be further insulated against cold by packing straw or fern through the branches. Evergreen boughs, pointed at the heavy end, and pushed into the ground around the base of the plant so that the branches shield the rhododendrons, make an excellent and quickly built cover. Pine or any of the cone-bearing trees may be used for this purpose.

Fill in Around Branches with Loose Straw or Fern Leaves

Heavy Mulch on Top of Roots

Rhododendrons (Continued)

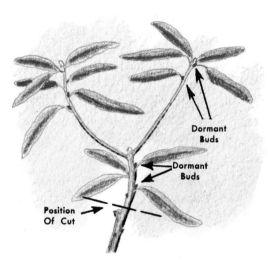

PRUNING

Gardeners are often confronted with the problem of a 'Pink Pearl' or similar large hybrid which has outgrown its position in the garden. They have no alternative but to prune, and this can be done without too much damage to the plant provided a little care is exercised. Rhododendron leaves occur in whorls at the end of each growth. In the axils of the leaves are growth buds which remain dormant unless they can be forced into growth by removing the stems beyond the point of their origin. By cutting back the stems to a whorl of leaves below, these buds are induced to break so that a plant might recover its growth the same spring.

The cutting is best done at flowering time and the plants should be watered heavily and given a little stimulant in the form of sulphate of ammonia, 2 ounces per square yard, thoroughly watered into the soil.

After flowering, the removal of old flower clusters will help conserve the plant's strength by preventing the setting of seed pods. In some hybrids the number of flower buds which form each year is often too many for the plant's health; a suggested measure of what to leave when disbudding is one bud to each square foot of leaf surface. By so doing, an even show of flowers is insured throughout the years and the plant is not weakened by the prodigality of its blossoms.

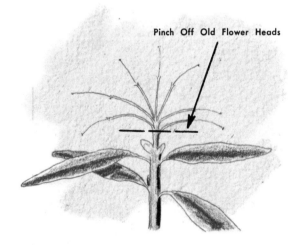

LS731

Rhododendron 'A. Bedford'

This is indeed a handsome plant with deep green foliage and strong growth. The tight, rounded trusses of lavender-blue appear in late May and the plant will become at least 7 feet high in ten years. Hardy to zero temperatures.

LS95

Rhododendron 'Betty Wormald'

The huge trusses and individually large flowers of rich carmine-pink combine with a compact habit to make this an especially desirable plant. It blooms in mid-May and is hardy to 5 degrees above zero. Height in ten years, 6 feet.

LS732

Rhododendron 'Album Grandiflorum'

A hardy hybrid out of *R. catawbiense* and considered by Arnold Arboretum to be one of the better varieties for northeast gardens. The rounded trusses become white when fully open and they appear in early May. The approximate height of the plant in ten years is five feet. Hardy to 15 degrees below zero.

LS549

Rhododendron 'Blue Peter'

The best in its color class. The habit is low, rarely exceeding 5 feet in height, with an eventual spread of about 7 feet. The rich, deep green, handsome leaves and large, rounded trusses of lavender-blue make this a distinctive hybrid which should be in every collection. It blooms in early May, has withstood down to zero temperatures and will become a bush 4 to 5 feet high in ten years.

Rhododendron 'Bowbells"

A very popular dwarf rhododendron with neat, rounded foliage and graceful bell-shaped flowers of rich pink. The young growth which follows is a striking bronze — resembling the new growth of *Pieris japonica*. Bowbells eventually becomes a compact, rounded shrub and in ten years should be about 4 feet high. It blooms in early May and is hardy to 5 degrees above zero.

LS730

Rhododendron 'Blue Tit'

A charming, dwarf, blue-flowering evergreen bush. Its height in ten years would be approximately 3 feet with a comparable spread in width. The small greyish-green leaves are literally hidden by clusters of lavender-blue flowers in April and the plants are most effectively used when planted en masse as a low hedge or group planting. Hardy to 5 degrees above zero.

LS686

LS622

Rhododendron 'Countess of Derby'

A hybrid between 'Pink Pearl' and 'Cynthia' combining the good qualities of both. A strong grower with beautiful foliage and superb trusses of rose-pink which appear in late May. Height in ten years would be about 6 feet and the plant has withstood 5 degrees above zero.

Rhododendron carolinianum album

This eastern American species is an excellent compact evergreen shrub which will withstand below zero temperatures. Its height in ten years would be about 3 feet and because of its rounded habit it is first class for landscaping where limited height is a must. The leaf size is much smaller than the conventional hybrid forms and it has a neat appearance enhanced by the rounded trusses of white flowers which appear in late May.

▽ Rhododendron 'Carita'

A lovely new hybrid from the famous Rothschild Gardens in England. The individually large flowers are carried in graceful trusses of from 12 to 13 flowers and open in late April. Beautiful foliage and hardy to 5 degrees above zero. Height in ten years 5 feet.

LS687

Rhododendron 'Britannia'

This popular variety has no equal as a low-growing scarlet rhododendron. The habit is compact and spreading, making it an ideal subject for landscaping the modern home. The flowers, which appear in early June, have a wonderful texture. This hybrid is hardy to 5 degrees above zero and will reach a height of about 4 feet in ten years.

LS729

LS88

Rhododendron 'Doncaster'

This slow-growing, compact grower blooms two weeks after 'Cynthia' and is a first-rate plant for foundation planting. Hardy to zero. Blooms in late May, and will reach a height of 4 feet in ten years.

LS728

LS726

Rhododendron 'Cynthia'

An old favorite and still a popular hybrid of strong growth and well-formed trusses of rosy red. This hybrid flowers in mid-May and is hardy to zero. Height in ten years 6 to 7 feet.

LS727

Rhododendron 'Goldsworth Yellow'   LS742

An attractive hybrid hardy to zero temperatures and blooming in late May. The opening flowers have a delightful apricot-pink shading becoming light yellow as they develop. Slow in growth, eventually 4 feet high in ten years.

LS89

Rhododendron 'Jean Marie de Montagu'

One of the best garden plants with a rounded, medium habit and dark green handsome leaves. The compact crimson trusses appear in mid-May and the plant attains a height of 5 feet in ten years. Hardy to 5 degrees above zero.

Rhododendron 'Earl of Athlone'

The clearest bright red in cultivation, with rounded, long-lasting trusses of excellent texture. It has an upright habit with good foliage and flowers in late April. The height in ten years is about 5 feet and the plant is hardy to 5 degrees above zero.

LS91

LS744

Rhododendron 'Loderi King George'

A magnificent rhododendron. The immense flowers, each measuring up to 7 inches across, are pure white and deliciously fragrant. It is a strong grower and will become a large shrub about 8 feet tall in ten years. To be seen at its best, the plants should be given high shade and protection from strong winds. Blooms in mid-May and has survived down to 5 degrees above zero.

LS745

Rhododendron 'Lady Bligh'

This fine hybrid has unusually beautiful flowers. When they first open the color is a deep strawberry red which changes, as they mature, to a rich pink with a paler center. The plant has a rounded habit and will become about 5 feet high in ten years. Blooms in May and is hardy to 5 degrees above zero.

LS92

Rhododendron 'Loder's White'

This is considered to be the best white rhododendron in cultivation for general garden use. The truss is well formed and the large, frilled flowers open with a tinge of pink and change to silvery-white. Blooms in early May, is hardy to 5 degrees above zero, and becomes a rounded shrub about 5 feet high in ten years.

LS749

Rhododendron 'Lord Roberts'

A popular variety with tight, round trusses of dark red blooms each of which has a distinctive marking in the throat. Blooms in late May and makes a compact bush up to 5 feet in ten years. Hardy to zero temperature.

LS750

Rhododendron 'Madame De Bruin'

A hardy hybrid which withstands zero temperatures and makes a free-blooming, compact plant to 5 feet in ten years. Blooms in mid-May.

Rhododendron 'Mars'

Here is an outstanding blood-red hybrid with large, deep green leaves and compact habit. This splendid rhododendron is hardy to below zero and produces its large trusses of striking flowers in late May. Its height in ten years would be about 4 feet.

LS751

Rhododendron 'Mrs. Furnival'

The demand for this fine variety has always been in excess of the supply. It is of slow growth and hardy to zero temperatures. The beautiful clear pink flowers have an attractive marking in the throat and, because of its compact, neat habit, it is an ideal plant for the small garden. Blooms in late May and its height in ten years would be about 4 feet.

LS753

LS90

Rhododendron 'Mrs. G. W. Leak'

A spectacular rhododendron of erect growth and dull green leaves. The large, cone-shaped trusses are an exciting shade of deep pink with a striking flare in the throat of each flower. Its height in ten years will be about 5 feet and the flowers appear in late May. Hardy to 5 degrees above zero.

Rhododendron 'Mrs. Chas. Pearson'

Immense flowers of blush mauve. A lovely hybrid with dark green foliage, eventually becoming a large shrub about 8 feet high in ten years. Blooms in mid-May and hardy to 5 degrees above zero.

LS546

Rhododendron 'Purple Splendor'

Without a doubt the finest purple rhododendron in cultivation. The rich purple flowers are enhanced by the deep markings on the upper petals. Blooms in early June and becomes a compact plant 4 feet high in ten years. Hardy to below zero.

LS94

LS743

Rhododendron 'Pink Pearl'

A very popular hybrid with huge trusses of lovely pink flowers. It blossoms in mid-May and attains a height of about 6 feet in ten years. Hardy to 5 degrees above zero.

LS746

LS547

Rhododendron 'Sappho'

A vigorous and hardy plant. This variety never fails to excite comment from all who see it in bloom. The deep green leaves are a perfect foil for the striking white trusses and each flower is highlighted by the deep maroon blotch within the throat. Hardy to zero and blooms in mid-May. Height in ten years 6 to 7 feet.

Rhododendron 'Trilby'

This low-growing hybrid with tight trusses of deep crimson flowers, has a neat compact habit and will attain a height of about 5 feet in ten years. The blossoms appear in late May and it is hardy to zero.

LS748

2370

Rhododendron 'Unique'

A tidy little plant eventually becoming a compact bush about 4 feet high in ten years. The neat habit and tight, rounded trusses of deep cream make this a great favorite for planting around the home. Blooms in late April and is hardy to 5 degrees above zero.

Rhododendron 'Unique' and 'Mrs. G. W. Leak'   LS752

LS23

Rhododendron 'Vulcan'

One of the best all-around red rhododendrons for general garden use. It has a medium compact habit, deep green leaves and numerous trusses of brick-red flowers. Hardy to zero and blooms in mid-May. In ten years, the plant should be from 4 to 5 feet high.

Rhododendron 'Unknown Warrior'

One of the earliest of the large-flowered rhododendrons to bloom. The trusses of bright red flowers are large, well formed, and appear in early April. Its habit is inclined to be spreading and its ultimate height in ten years would be about 4 feet. Hardy to 5 degrees above zero.

LS98

LS788

LS789

Rhododendron 'Alice'

This popular hybrid is preferred by some to 'Pink Pearl' because of a more compact habit and a richer color in the truss. The tall cones of rich pink appear in mid-May and the approximate height of the plant should be about 6 feet in ten years. It is hardy to about zero.

Rhododendron 'America'

Here is a strong-growing Dutch hybrid with freely-produced, rounded trusses of bright red. It blooms in mid-May and is hardy to about 15 degrees below zero. Its estimated height in ten years should be about 6 feet.

Rhododendron 'Beauty of Littleworth'

This spectacular *R. griffithianum* hybrid becomes a tall shrub, approximately 8 feet in 10 years. The white flowers, speckled carmine, appear in early May and are carried in huge built-up trusses. It is hardy to about 5 degrees above zero.

Rhododendron 'Dr. H. C. Dresselhuys'

A vigorous-growing hybrid, possibly 8 feet high in ten years and bearing crimson-red trusses in late May. It is hardy to 15 degrees below zero.

LS790

LS791

Rhododendron 'General Eisenhower'

LS792

One of the new race of hardy hybrids introduced by Kluis of Holland. It is strong-growing and should reach a height of about 8 feet in ten years. The huge trusses of cherry red are at their best in late May and the plant is hardy to about 10 degrees below zero.

Rhododendron 'Queen Mary'

This new Dutch hybrid with handsome leathery foliage bears large, rounded trusses of deep pink in late May. It is hardy to about 10 degrees below zero and should attain a height of about 6 feet in 10 years.

Rhododendron 'Jan Dekens'

LS93

This Dutch hybrid has beautiful foliage and very large trusses of rich pink flowers which are attractively fringed, in mid-May. Height in ten years about 6 feet; hardy to about 5 degrees below zero.

Rhododendron 'Mrs. W. C. Slocock'

A dwarf, compact hybrid with a neat habit. The rounded trusses are comprised of many apricot-pink flowers which eventually shade to creamy yellow when fully open. Blooms in late May; hardy to about zero, with a height of about 4 feet in 10 years.

LS793

LS794

CONIFEROUS EVERGREENS

Section 70

CONIFEROUS EVERGREENS

Introduction

THERE ARE estimated to be about 930 distinct species and varieties of coniferous evergreens in cultivation in the United States. While this list is made up of 33 genera, or family groups, we find more than two-thirds of the total represented by only six of these genera which total 636 as follows:

Junipers 148
Pines 145
Spruces 108
Arborvitae 91
Firs 87
Yews 57

The number of forms is constantly changing as new varieties are added and some old ones are discontinued and disappear. This brief appraisal will show how limited is the assortment, as compared to the whole, that any book can illustrate.

America is a large country. Temperatures run from mild to severe. Altitude, presence of mountains, prevailing wind conditions, sudden changes in temperature and other conditions make it impossible to say that any certain variety will survive in any given locality. The illustrations in this book represent a cross section of varieties, showing the various habits of growth and including several forms which are suitable only for a mild climate.

For example, the coniferous evergreens of southern California and northern Florida are a distinct group some of which cannot be used elsewhere. Some others in northern California, Washington and Oregon include forms which are not suited to the middle west. Few coniferous evergreens are grown on the Texas Gulf Coast and almost none in southern Florida. Certain forms are used in New England which are not hardy or satisfactory in Illinois. The great plains states are restricted to only a few varieties.

Thus it will be seen that anyone contemplating planting should consult a reputable nurseryman to find what local conditions prevail and just what varieties may be expected to survive in any area. This is very important.

Fortunately there are interesting conifers suitable for most areas of the United States. Planters in the south may regret not being able to grow the Colorado Blue Spruce, whereas others in the north may wish to grow the Deodar Cedar, but compensations will be found for all such limitations.

By confining the choice of materials to those forms which have proven satisfactory in any given locality, the trees may be better expected to thrive over a long period.

In the making of color plates many considerations are involved. Most coniferous evergreens exhibit color changes throughout the year. Particularly in the colder climates trees will take on a different color during the winter months. Some trees which are normally deep green will develop a yellowish cast when growing in impoverished soil. On the other hand trees such as yews will develop extremely lustrous green when planted in heavy shade. Trees that have been carefully

Coniferous Evergreens (Continued)

pruned and well taken care of look entirely different from those which have been neglected. Thus it will be seen that no single color plate can represent all the forms or colors which any tree may on occasion show.

The term "evergreen" derives from the fact that leaves remain intact and green during the winter months, and these trees are known as "conifers" because the seeds of many genera are borne in cone-like structures.

STRUCTURE OF FLOWERING PROCESS OF CONIFERS

Thirteen genera of coniferous evergreens are illustrated in this book and are briefly described as follows:

FIRS (Abies)

Fir trees, with their impressive size and rich foliage are of great value in landscaping. They have a shapely, symmetrical form and when properly selected for their site are long lived. In old age they develop into majestic subjects. Of scattered natural occurrence, some of the best species derive from the Cascade Mountains, from Colorado, from Japan and from the borders of the Mediterranean Sea. It is a characteristic of firs that they thrive in a moist, well-drained soil and grow best in a humid climate.

CEDAR (Cedrus)

Of the three well known and closely related cedars, the Lebanon, Atlas and Deodar, none is native to America. These are the only true cedars, this common name being widely misapplied to many other trees. All three make large-growing trees which need room for development. They are used extensively in the southern states from Virginia and Tennessee southward and along the entire length of the Pacific Coast, but are not hardy where the temperature is severely cold or where hot summer winds are prevalent.

FALSECYPRESS (Chamaecyparis)

Of the five species of falsecypress which are native to North America and Japan, three are illustrated. Most of these are naturally narrow-upright and relatively tall growing but there is a great variation of form in some species, so that more than forty horticultural varieties are in cultivation. Many of them make small, bushy or spreading trees with fine-needled, delicate, and vari-colored foliage.

CRYPTOMERIA (Cryptomeria)

There is but one species of cryptomeria in common use. The form which makes a medium-sized tree of upright compact habit, and is extensively used as an ornamental tree on the Pacific Coast and throughout the south, is rarely planted in the middle west.

JUNIPER (Juniperus)

The hundreds of horticultural varieties of junipers would require an entire book to illustrate and describe. Some varieties are of local interest and others are planted over most of the country. No other genus of coniferous evergreens hardy in the

Coniferous Evergreens (Continued)

north includes such a large number of forms resulting from seedling variation. They range in habit from narrow, spire-like forms to those that trail on the ground. Gardeners almost anywhere in the United States may use junipers in great variety.

INCENSE CEDAR (Libocedrus)

A native west coast evergreen which attains great size. It is used almost exclusively on the north Pacific Coast, just occasionally in the east. Only the native species is commonly planted.

PINE (Pinus)

To many people "pine" is synonymous with "coniferous evergreen," or "Christmas tree." But specifically, of course, it applies to an extensive genus of long-needled evergreens of which more than seventy-five species occur throughout the world. With the exception of some dwarfs, pines are among the taller, more massive conifers. On the Pacific Coast are many native forms not used elsewhere, but some kinds of them may be grown in every state of the union.

SPRUCE (Picea)

Spruces comprise one of the most important genera of coniferous evergreens for planters in the cooler sections of the country. They are primarily cold-loving trees and do not thrive where it is too warm. There are about thirty species and numerous horticultural varieties. The Norway Spruce has produced a great many dwarf forms, but most native species make tall, majestic specimens. Most of the forest conifers of the north are either spruce or pine. The Colorado spruce, because of its bright blue color, is a great favorite in cooler climates.

YEW PODOCARPUS (Podocarpus)

Podocarpus is an extensive genus belonging to the yew family. Several species are native to Africa and other parts of the southern hemisphere. Only two or three varieties are commonly grown in the southern United States. It is not hardy in the north.

YEW (Taxus)

During the past twenty years interest in yews has increased to a greater extent than in any other group of conifers. So many new forms have been introduced that there is some confusion and duplication of varieties. The habit of growth runs from low spreading and round ball-shaped to columnar and tree-like forms. They are for the most part trees of modest stature and are widely used in landscape work, being one of the best evergreens for shady places. They do not do well in the deep south.

ARBORVITAE (Thuja)

There are five species of arborvitae of which two are native to North America. The American arborvitae is very extensively used both in its natural form and in its many varieties. In former years, before the yews became generally available, arborvitae was even more widely used than at present and its flat, fern-like foliage is familiar to everyone. Oriental arborvitae, of which 'Berckmanns Golden' is a variety, is less hardy in the north than the American species.

DOUGLAS FIR (Pseudotsuga)

This tree resembles a fir with a long-pointed terminal bud. The single species reaches a great size in natural stands of the

Coniferous Evergreens *(Continued)*

Cascade Mountains. A somewhat smaller strain is native to Colorado and is the form grown over most of the country as the Pacific Coast strain does not grow far away from its native habitat.

GIANT SEQUOIA *(Sequoiadendron)*

This is one of two species of sequoia which were once wide-spread in ages past. Now confined in its native stand to western slopes of the Sierra Nevada Mountains in California it is one of the largest growing of all the evergreens and very long lived. A fast grower and an excellent specimen in localities where it is suited to the climate.

Cultural Suggestions

When evergreens come from the nursery there is an earth ball around the roots which is enclosed with burlap and twine. The trees should be planted without removing the burlap. It is not even neces-

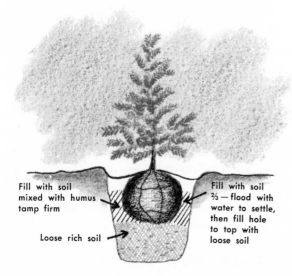

Fill with soil mixed with humus tamp firm

Fill with soil ⅔ — flood with water to settle, then fill hole to top with loose soil

Loose rich soil

sary to cut the string as it quickly disappears in the ground. Dig the hole somewhat larger than the earth ball, so that

you will have several inches of loose soil at the bottom of the ball and around it. Never force the earth ball into a small hole, especially if the soil is hard or very poor. If rubble or very poor soil is found, dig out and replace with good garden soil which is loose and free from hard clay, stones and rubble. It is also a big help to mix about one-fourth of peat moss with the soil which you put back in the hole. This provides a good bed for the development of new roots. For fertilizer use organic compost made from rotted leaves or any fertilizer made from processed cattle manure. Recommended commercial fertilizers are often helpful, but do not use close to roots as burning may result.

Fertilizing may be done once a year either with a root feeder or by digging fertilizer into the top soil. Extra care in fertilization will pay in better results and more luxuriant growth.

WATERING

In providing water for evergreens it is important that we understand the effect which improper watering has upon root growth. Intermittent light watering which does not penetrate more than a few inches below the soil surface does more harm than good. It causes the roots to turn upward, seeking water, so that they are more than ever dependent on continuous moisture in the top layer of soil. By a soaking process, taking the nozzle off the hose, perhaps using a burlap sack tied around the end, you can allow the water to seep into the ground as long as it will be absorbed. This will place moisture down below the trees where it should be.

There is danger of watering too much under conditions where drainage is poor.

Coniferous Evergreens (Continued)

If there is hard clay, or other conditions which prevent the water from draining away, you should first place gravel or cinders beneath the tree, and provide an outlet from this material to guard against water standing and rotting the roots.

Newly planted trees need to be watered at least once a week or ten days, but established trees need watering only under conditions of extreme drought.

CULTIVATING

The maintenance of a dust mulch in the cultivated area around newly planted trees helps to conserve moisture in the soil. Trees can easily be kept in good condition if the work is done with a scratch hoe at frequent intervals during the summer months. Such cultivation eliminates weeds which not only look bad but also provide a place for insects and fungus diseases to become established.

PRUNING

The need for pruning arises from the fact that few trees grow in nature exactly as we wish to have them grow in a landscape planting. When evergreens are used in foundation plantings or other restricted areas, it is necessary that their growth be held back so that their period of usefulness may be prolonged.

Pruning to produce symmetrical or compact growth habit is particularly needed with the medium and dwarf forms commonly a part of residential plantings.

Evergreens may also suffer from damage to leader shoots, causing uneven growth, or branches may be injured from diverse causes. Trees are individual in character so that when it may be necessary to develop trees of similar habit, some must necessarily be pruned and shaped more than others.

For formal effect and symmetry, as well as for similarity of habit, it may be necessary to shape trees by pruning. Coniferous evergreen trees should be maintained in a shape and form in proper relation to their surroundings and this fact accounts in a large measure for the need of pruning. When used as free-growing specimens for decorative, shade or screen purposes where space is not limiting, no pruning of such trees is necessary.

Pruning also provides a means of re-

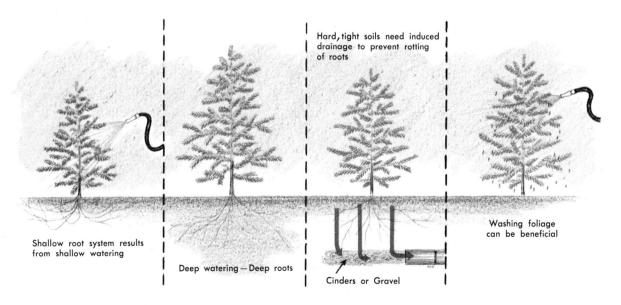

Shallow root system results from shallow watering

Deep watering — Deep roots

Hard, tight soils need induced drainage to prevent rotting of roots

Cinders or Gravel

Washing foliage can be beneficial

Coniferous Evergreens (Continued)

plenishing the growth. When trees become weakened or have too many branches, their condition may often be improved by cutting back their growth and thereby encouraging the dormant buds and inner branches of the tree to develop.

Trees which have scale-like foliage and many small branches, such as cypress, junipers, arborvitae and hemlock, can be trimmed without much regard for dormant buds. They make growth from so many points and break buds so extensively that it is not essential to consider the place of cut.

In pruning trees which grow in definite layers of branches such as pines, spruces, cedars and similar forms, we should regard the pruning in relation to the dormant buds, so that half-removed annual growths will not be left as inactive stubs to die back to their point of origin.

The time of year for pruning is of secondary importance. Pruning goes on in most nurseries at all seasons whenever time may be found for it. Generally speak-

ing it is better to prune in early summer so that buds can develop during the ensuing growing season.

The ideal pruning equipment for soft-foliaged trees is a sharp pruning knife. Where it is necessary to remove woody branches which cannot be readily taken off with a pruning knife, the use of pruning shears is recommended. In general it may be said that plantings will live for many years and remain in an attractive form longer if a definite program of pruning is followed. Within the limitations cited above you cannot injure your trees through pruning. DO NOT BE AFRAID to prune when pruning is needed.

It is not good practice to prune evergreens into shapes too far removed from their natural habit. For example, do not try to make Norway Spruce into a ball-shaped tree or to train an Irish Juniper into a creeping form. Except for the topiary addict the art of pruning is to be considered not as a creative operation, but as a corrective one.

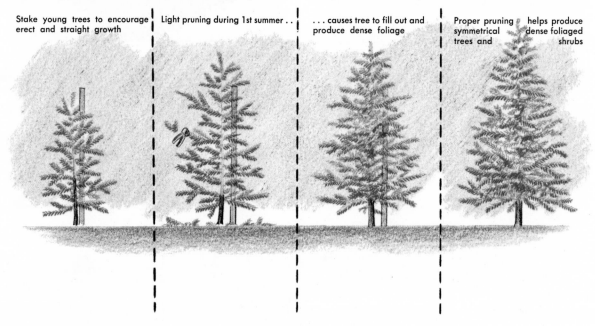

Stake young trees to encourage erect and straight growth

Light pruning during 1st summer . .

. . . causes tree to fill out and produce dense foliage

Proper pruning helps produce symmetrical trees and dense foliaged shrubs

Coniferous Evergreen Planting LS893

Juniperus horizontalis plumosa (8)
ANDORRA JUNIPER

A low, spreading shrub growing 18 inches to 2 feet high and spreading as much as 8 to 10 feet. Foliage is greyish green in summer turning to purple in autumn and winter. Hardy to 30 degrees below zero. Excellent for use as a border for taller trees and as a ground cover for cut banks and hillsides.

Juniperus horizontalis (10)
BAR HARBOR JUNIPER

A low, spreading shrub with attractive soft blue coloring. One of the most widely used forms. Hardy below zero degrees.

Juniperus sabina tamariscifolia (7)
TAMARIX SAVIN JUNIPER

See page 70-5 for description.

Juniperus chinensis 'Japonica Aurea' (4)
GOLDEN JAPANESE JUNIPER

Syn. *J. chinensis 'Plumosa Aurea'*

A low-growing plant spreading its branches in feathery arches. May attain a height of 7 to 9 feet with a spread of 5 to 7 feet after several years. Young foliage is a golden yellow. Hardy to about 20 degrees below zero.

Juniperus sabina (3)
SAVIN JUNIPER

A low, multi-branched shrub eventually growing 6 to 8 feet tall with about the same spread. Its spreading, upturned branches are densely clothed in dark scale-like green foliage. Thrives in soils of high lime content but is not restricted to such. Hardy to about 15 degrees below zero.

Juniperus virginiana tripartita (6)
FOUNTAIN EASTERN RED CEDAR

A dwarf spreading form with upright habit. Dense needle-shaped leaves of somewhat greyish green. Rarely attains a height of more than 6 feet with a spread of 8 to 10 feet. Hardy to about 30 degrees below zero.

Cedrus atlantica glauca (1)
BLUE ATLAS CEDAR

See page 70-2 for description.

Pinus mugo mughus (2)
MUGHO PINE

See page 70-8 for description.

Chamaecyparis lawsoniana erecta 'Elwoodi' (5)
ELWOOD CYPRESS

A dense, slow growing shrub of upright columnar habit to about 8 feet tall. Very attractive with dark bluish-green foliage. At its best in moist climates. Hardy to about 5 degrees below zero.

Taxus baccata 'Washingtoni' (11)
WASHINGTON YEW

A wide spreading plant growing 6 to 8 feet tall at maturity with a spread of 5 to 8 feet. Foliage is a golden yellow more strongly pronounced on underside of leaves. Excellent for screening and background material for smaller plants. Hardy to about 5 degrees below zero.

Thuja orientalis 'Aurea Nana' (9)
BERKMANNS GOLDEN ARBORVITAE

See page 70-11 for description.

LS894

Cedrus deodara
DEODAR CEDAR

A fast-growing cedar from the Himalaya Mountains which is widely planted throughout the west, particularly in the southern part, and succeeds in milder zones elsewhere. Grows in a broad pyramidal manner to 50 feet or more, with open sweeping branches clothed with frosty blue-green needles. One of the most satisfactory of conifers for areas of low humidity and some alkalinity. Hardy to about 5 degrees.

Abies concolor
WHITE FIR

Large, conical western mountain tree of symmetrical shape, growing rather slowly to 100 feet or more, but seldom over 50 feet in cultivation. Very good-looking blue-green conifer which is regularly cut for Christmas trees. Not very well suited for hot low-humidity areas. Sun or part shade. Hardy below zero degrees.

LS896

LS895

Abies pinsapo glauca
BLUE SPANISH FIR

Slow-growing pyramidal tree ultimately reaching 70 or 80 feet. Short, stiff needles of frosty blue-green are spaced uniformly around each branch in this variety. Somewhat better adapted to hot dry conditions than *A. concolor*. Hardy to about zero degrees.

Cedrus atlantica glauca
BLUE ATLAS CEDAR

Grows rather slowly into a tall, broadly conical tree of open habit (ultimately 75 feet or more) with irregular flattened branches. Unusual color is provided by the tufts of short needles, intense silvery-blue in color, which crowd closely along each branch. Hardy to zero.

LS897

LS898

LS899

Chamaecyparis pisifera 'Yellowthread'
GOLDEN SAWARA CYPRESS

Very showy small form with spreading branches and a rather lacy habit. Extremely slow growing, seldom over 6 feet tall in cultivation and with equivalent mound-like spread. Most attractive when new growth shows a bright gold-green color. Sun or part shade. Hardy below zero degrees.

Chamaecyparis lawsoniana erecta
ERECT LAWSON CYPRESS

Very beautiful, slow-growing, long-lived conifer, rather slender and erect in habit and very desirable for its dense foliage of bright green. May ultimately reach 80 feet or more but is more often seen as a garden specimen 10 to 12 feet tall. Sun or part shade. Hardy to about 10 degrees.

Chamaecyparis lawsoniana 'Allumi'
BLUE LAWSON CYPRESS

Makes a compact, columnar specimen, growing very slowly. May reach 30 feet or more in height with a spread of 8 to 10 feet, but not for many years. Highly prized for its very dense attractive foliage of metallic blue-green. Sun or part shade. Hardy to about 5 degrees.

LS900

LS901

LS917

Juniperus communis hibernica
IRISH JUNIPER

A neat, small, narrow, very erect juniper with compact blue-green foliage. Spreads to 1½ to 2 feet in diameter and is seldom over 6 to 7 feet in height. Useful evergreen for accent. Sun or part shade. Hardy below zero degrees.

Chamaecyparis obtusa
HINOKI CYPRESS

A slow-growing tree 10 to 30 feet tall and spreading 5 to 20 feet. Branches are densely covered with flat sprays of rich green, scale-like leaves. Pyramidal, with branches pendulous at tips. Distinct and highly decorative and at its best in moist air of cool coastal areas. Tolerates heat and cold. Hardy to about 20 degrees below zero.

Juniperus chinensis 'Pfitzeriana'
PFITZER JUNIPER

Forms a fountain-like mass of bluish-green foliage, with its wide-spreading horizontal branches reaching from 6 to 8 feet in height and as much across. Grows readily in almost any soil. Sun or part shade. Hardy well below zero degrees.

LS902

LS492

Juniperus squamata meyeri
MEYER SINGLESEED JUNIPER

Some branches are erect while others grow horizontally, then angle abruptly upward to give the plants an irregular and informal outline. Grows to a height of 6 feet or more but may vary considerably in spread. The foliage is dense and very bright in color, a striking blue-green with glints of silver and even some pink tones in new growth. An interesting conifer for partly shaded spots. Hardy below zero degrees.

Juniperus chinensis 'Torulosa'
TWISTED JUNIPER

Makes a picturesque semi-dwarf juniper of rich dark green, which grows erectly to 10 or 12 feet. Can be kept lower, more spreading, to 5 or 6 feet, with training. Branches naturally grow in a twisted, contorted manner which gives the shrub its distinctive character. Often used as an accent plant with broad-leaved ornamentals; also as a tubbed specimen. Sun or part shade. Hardy below zero degrees.

LS876

Juniperus excelsa stricta Syn. *J. chinensis pyramidalis*
SPINY GREEK JUNIPER

A small, slow-growing tree to about 5 feet tall with a spread of 3 feet. Dense growth of spiny blue foliage and formal, narrow column or shape. Prefers a dry sunny location. Hardy to about 10 degrees below zero.

Juniperus sabina tamariscifolia
TAMARIX SAVIN JUNIPER

One of the best of the junipers where a low spreading type is needed. Makes a complete mound of grey-green foliage, spreading its irregular, pointed branches to 10 feet or more. Seldom exceeds 18 inches in height. Grows readily in almost any soil or climate. Full sun. Hardy below zero degrees.

1784

2039

LS444

Juniperus virginiana 'Hilli'
HILL'S DUNDEE REDCEDAR

Changing color of the foliage is one of the interesting features of this variety. The perfectly symmetrical cone-like plant is densely clothed with foliage, pale bluish-green when new, changing to striking plum-like hues in the fall. Grows to 10 or 12 feet in height with a spread of about 3 feet at the base. Hardy below zero degrees.

2300

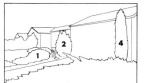

Coniferous Evergreen Planting

1. **Juniperus sabina tamariscifolia**
   TAMARIX SAVIN JUNIPER (See page 70-5 for description)
2. **Juniperus chinensis 'Torulosa'**
   TWISTED JUNIPER (See page 70-5 for description)
3. **Juniperus chinensis 'Pfitzeriana'**
   PFITZER JUNIPER (See page 70-4 for description)
4. **Chamaecyparis lawsoniana erecta 'Elwoodi'**
   ELWOOD CYPRESS (See page 70-1 for description)

Libocedrus decurrens
INCENSE CEDAR

A native of mountainous areas of the West Coast which makes a handsome long-lived tree, ultimately from 40 to 60 feet or more tall. Makes an extremely dense pyramid of rich green foliage, always neat and compact, regardless of its age. The foliage has a clean aromatic fragrance when crushed. Grows easily in almost any soil and is relatively heat tolerant. Hardy to zero degrees.

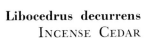

2385

LS886

Picea pungens glauca
COLORADO BLUE SPRUCE

Beautiful, perfectly symmetrical tree, broadly pyramidal, reaching ultimately to 80 feet or more. Has stiff branches and compact needles which are a striking silvery-blue the year around. Grows slowly and is not too well suited to dry arid conditions. Hardy below zero.

LS887

Picea glauca albertiana 'Conica'
DWARF ALBERTA SPRUCE

Tiny tree of perfect conical shape, each branch thickly covered with short fine needles. New growth is bright green, becoming silvery with age. Grows only an inch or so each year and probably will not reach 10 feet in a lifetime. Good tub specimen but best suited to cooler more moist areas. Hardy well below zero.

Picea abies
NORWAY SPRUCE

One of the fastest growing of the spruces, making a broadly pyramidal tree with rather stiff branches, densely clothed with thick short needles. Tends to become irregular and somewhat sparse with age. May reach 150 feet under favorable conditions, but mature garden specimens usually range from 60 to 75 feet. Widely planted for windbreaks or single specimen in northern and eastern parts of the U.S. Hardy below zero degrees.

Picea abies 'Nidiformis'
NEST BLACK NORWAY SPRUCE

Extremely slow growing with a very dense foliage head and a thick nest-like mass of branches. May get 2 feet tall and 4 feet across, but not for many years since it grows only 2 inches or less a year. Grows best in cool moist areas. Hardy below zero degrees.

LS888

LS491

Pinus koraiensis
KOREAN PINE

LS881

Dense, broad, pyramidal tree, growing ultimately to 75 feet or more but more often seen as a garden specimen under 20 feet. Makes a handsome tree with long 3- to 4-inch needles, glossy dark green, silvery margined. Because of its slow growth it makes a good, hardy, small garden pine. Hardy below zero degrees.

Pinus radiata ⟱
MONTEREY PINE

One of the fastest-growing of all pines to 60 feet or more. Has long, bright green needles and when young is pyramidal in shape. Becomes an irregular round-headed specimen with age, spreading to 30 feet or so. Good coastal tree. Hardy to about 10 degrees.

Pinus mugo mughus
MUGHO PINE

A shrubby dwarf pine which remains densely compact and symmetrical from infancy through old age. Seldom over 4 to 6 feet tall, but often more spreading. Dark green, closely-spaced needles make it a fine all-year ornamental. An excellent pot specimen. Plant in full sun. Very hardy.

2259

Pinus griffithi
HIMALAYAN PINE

LS882

A tree of broad, open pyramidal habit growing to upwards of 60 feet tall and spreading 15 to 18 feet, with slender, drooping foliage of greyish or bluish green. Hardy to 10 degrees below zero.

LS883

Podocarpus macrophylla maki
LS875
SHRUBBY YEW PODOCARPUS

Low, shrubby, rather stiff plant with erect branches covered thickly with handsome, narrow, 4-inch leaves of shiny dark green. Seldom over 5 feet tall but height and spread vary according to training. Excellent pot or tub specimen in sun or shade. Hardy to about 20 degrees.

LS877

Podocarpus elongata
FERN PODOCARPUS

Graceful, slow growing little tree with spreading irregular branches densely clothed with soft, lacy, fern-like foliage. May get to 30 feet but is more often 15 feet or so tall with about same spread. Sun or part shade. Hardy to about 18 degrees.

Pseudotsuga taxifolia
DOUGLAS FIR

Native timber tree of the moist mountain slopes from California north to British Columbia. Grows in pyramidal shape, ranging from 75 to over 200 feet in height. Short needles, rich green, sometimes with a bluish cast, crowd closely around each branch. Grows well in most soils but dislikes hot, dry lowland areas. Inland forms are hardy well below zero degrees.

LS890

Sequoiadendron (Sequoia) giganteum
GIANT SEQUOIA

The famous California "Big Trees" of the Sierra Nevada Mountains, the oldest and largest of all living things. In the garden it makes a perfectly symmetrical dense cone of blue-green foliage, staying well within "small garden" size for many years. Grows easily except in drier and coldest areas. Hardy below zero degrees.

LS892

LS879

Taxus baccata 'Fastigiata Aurea'
GOLDEN IRISH YEW

Very similar to the green Irish Yew in habit and requirements, but in this the new growth is a distinctive golden color. Grows a little more slowly than the green variety and is perhaps slightly less hardy.

Taxus media 'Hicksi'
HICKS YEW

Narrow columnar yew with vertical branches thickly covered with dark green closely-set needles. Grows rather slowly to 8 or 10 feet with a spread of perhaps 4 feet, remaining a rich lush green color all year. Prefers moist, rich soil and partial shade. Hardy below zero degrees.

LS880

Thuja orientalis 'Aurea Nana' LS889
BERKMANNS GOLDEN ARBORVITAE

A tightly foliaged, perfectly symmetrical conifer, conical when young but gradually becoming more globular with age. Ultimately grows to about 6 feet in height with a spread of 4 to 5 feet. Throughout much of the year the dark green foliage is interestingly tipped with golden yellow. Grows easily almost anywhere. Hardy to zero degrees.

Taxus baccata 'Fastigiata' ▷
IRISH YEW

Grows slowly in a very upright, narrow manner, making a tall, dense column of dark green. May ultimately attain about 20 feet in height but not for many years. Usually tends to be more spreading (3 feet or so) at the top, less at the base. Grows best in part shade, good soil and plenty of moisture. Hardy below zero degrees.

Thuja occidentalis 'Douglasi Pyramidalis'

Syn. *T. occidentalis pyramidalis*
PYRAMIDAL ARBORVITAE

One of the older ornamental favorites of compact pyramidal shape. Many ultimately reach 18 to 20 feet in height with a spread of 5 to 8 feet. Ascending branches of bright green foliage. Hardy to 20 degrees below zero.

Taxus baccata LS878
◁ ENGLISH YEW

Very slow growing. After many years and under favorable conditions, may make a tree 25 to 40 feet tall, with a low spreading crown to 20 feet or more. It is more familiar as a somewhat fountain-like garden specimen, 8 or 10 feet tall, covered thickly with shiny dark-green needles. Sun or shade, good soil, and moisture. Hardy to zero degrees.

LS498

Thuja occidentalis pumila
LITTLE GEM ARBORVITAE

A small, rounded, very compact arborvitae with dark green foliage. Maximum height is about 24 inches with spread only slightly greater. Makes a good small formal plant for the garden or as a tubbed specimen. Prefers good soil, plenty of moisture, and shelter from drying winds. Hardy to about zero degrees.

LS607

Taxus cuspidata
JAPANESE YEW

Handsome, spreading plant growing 6 to 8 feet in height and spreading up to 10 feet. Rather slow-growing. Has an informal graceful habit with branches thickly covered with large shiny needles. Fine permanent foreground shrub, even in almost full shade. Will tolerate a good deal of moisture. Hardy to about zero degrees.

Thuja occidentalis 'Woodwardi'
WOODWARD ARBORVITAE

One of the most popular arborvitaes of globe form eventually growing 8 to 10 feet tall and wide, maintaining a compact, well-rounded shape. Dark green foliage. Hardy to about 20 degrees below zero.

Thuja occidentalis globosa
GLOBE ARBORVITAE

A compact globe form with slender branches of bright green foliage. Ultimately reaching 2 to 3 feet in height and spread. Prefers rich soil and moisture. Hardy to about 10 degrees below zero.

LS884

LS885

VINES AND GROUND COVERS

Section 80

VINES AND GROUND COVERS

Introduction

A DICTIONARY definition of the word "vine" may be as follows: "Any plant with long slender stems that trails or creeps on the ground or climbs by winding itself around a support or by holding fast with tendrils or other means."

Correct as it may be this generalization fails to indicate just how diverse are the habits or how very many "families" of the plant world are represented among the so-called "vines."

Horticulturally, there are deciduous vines, evergreen sorts, hardy ones, frost-tender kinds, slow growing, fast growing, perennial and annual types. Functionally, some are densely-foliaged and opaque, others are light and airy for delicate tracery effects. Some have glossy leaves which reflect light, others have dull foliage which absorbs it. There are large vines and small, kinds that afford protection against hot summer sun or prevailing winds, others that require protection from the same elements. There are flowering vines to provide as much garden drama as any plant can.

There are, finally, those vines which spread over the ground to make a thick undulating mantle of foliage and are referred to as "ground covers." In short, there are many vines offering all sorts of opportunities for increasing the beauty of landscape plantings.

It is important that vines be chosen with care, the right one for the right place. Many of them grow with great rapidity and can soon cover a designated area of fence, wall or trellis. But they can become too large, also. In addition to size, one should consider exposure, color, texture for architectural balance and, finally, the kinds best suited for the types of surfaces they are intended to cover. The method by which it climbs or clings is usually the determining factor here.

Twining Vines

There are vines which literally "wrap" themselves around a vertical support. Some twist to the right, others to the left. If young shoots are started around their support in the proper direction of rotation, growth will be faster. Once given a start, they usually take care of themselves, except for an occasional thinning of the heavier-growing types. Typical examples are Carolina jessamine *(Gelsemium)*, Chinese gooseberry *(Actinidia)*, honeysuckle, silver fleece vine, Kudzu vine, wisterias, etc.

Vines Self-Supporting by Means of Rootlets or Discs

These are vines which by means of rootlets or suction-cup discs will cling to most any surface, providing their own means of attachment. From these one may choose the vines which are best suited to grow against masonry, stucco or stone work where special supports are difficult to provide. A few of the better-known vines in this category are the true ivies *(Hedera)*, Boston ivy, climbing hydrangea, several of the *Euonymus,* and in warmer areas, the catclaw trumpet and the Mexican blood trumpet vine *(Phaedranthus)*.

Vines Clinging by Means of Tendrils

In this group are vines well suited to growing on a lattice, wire fence, trellis, or anything having horizontal members

Vines and Ground Covers (Continued)

around which the vine can twine its tendrils. By contracting, the tendrils actually draw the vine close to its support. Well-known examples in this class are members of the *Ampelopsis* family, including Virginia creeper, queen's wreath *(Antigonon)*, clematis varieties, the passion vine, and perhaps the best known of all — many varieties of grape, both ornamental and fruiting varieties.

Fast-growing Vines

Some vines grow with great rapidity and are capable of providing a screen or covering an unsightly object in a very short time. A few better-known, fast-growing deciduous varieties are Kudzu vine, trumpet creeper *(Campsis)*, grape vines *(Vitis)*, wisterias, Boston ivy, Virginia creeper, and some of the clematis varieties. Evergreen kinds include catclaw creeper *(Doxantha)*, Japanese honeysuckle, English and Algerian ivy, creeping fig, blood trumpet, *Distictis* and bougainvillea.

Vines Having Showy Flowers

Many vines are extremely ornamental because of their profuse flowering, and they are found among the deciduous as well as the evergreen sorts, among the fast growing and also the slow growing kinds. Some of these are familiar sights in all parts of the country since they grow and bloom well under widely varying conditions. A few, including most of the clematis varieties, require winter chilling and special soil conditions to bloom their best. The biggest single factor determining adaptability, however, is hardiness. Many of the most spectacular vines in cultivation are from the tropics and are suitable only for the mild-wintered areas. Some of these bloom almost throughout the year.

Popular flowering vines include wisterias, clematis, honeysuckle, queen's wreath, silver fleece vine, climbing roses, trumpet creeper *(Campsis)*, etc. Notable sorts for milder areas are: bougainvilleas, passion vine, jasmine, Burmese honeysuckle, cup of gold, violet trumpet vine, Mexican blood trumpet, sky flower and star jasmine.

Vines for Shade

While most of the vines, particularly those which flower heavily, need sun or at least part sun, there are a few varieties which thrive in shade. Among these are clematis, English ivy, Carolina jessamine *(Gelsemium)*, honeysuckle and star jasmine *(Trachelospermum)*.

Culture

PLANTING OF VINES

Vines should be planted just as carefully as any other shrub or tree. Good soil, good drainage and an adequate supply of plant food are just as important. In fact, some of the vines which grow very rapidly may be even more demanding of water and fertilizer than other plants. Generally, any good garden soil is suitable for vines. However, some may require that soils on the alkaline side be corrected if they are to produce their best flowers.

Since vines are often grown in a rather restricted space, a little extra care in keeping the soil open, aerated and fertile often pays big dividends in plant performance.

In the planting of deciduous vines, a good rule is to set the plant to the same depth as in the nursery. Usually a difference in the character of the bark, often in its color, will make the original planting depth clearly visible. Make some allowance for settling, particularly in loose or

Vines and Ground Covers (Continued)

sandy loam. Firm the soil well around the plant and settle it to remove all air pockets by running water slowly into the planting basin.

Many vines, especially the evergreen ones, are sold growing in containers — tin cans, clay pots or something of the sort. Again, the same rule regarding depth applies, i.e., set the top of the soil as it comes from the container even with the soil level at the planting site.

Plants in clay pots may be removed by turning the pot upside down and tapping its edge gently on the workbench or some similar object. Be sure to hold one hand over the soil in the pot before tapping.

If the vine is in one of the gallon cans used extensively in the south and west, split the can on opposite sides with a tin snips, chisel or stout knife and carefully lift out the ball of soil.

SPLIT CAN ON OPPOSITE SIDES
DO NOT BREAK EARTH BALL WHILE HANDLING

Larger plants in square or round 5-gallon cans may be handled in the same manner.

Be sure the support on which your vine is to be trained is sturdy enough to keep the vine from toppling when exposed to heavy wind. No vines are entirely self-supporting and the weight of a big foliage mass can be considerable.

TRAINING OF VINES

A little help in directing the growth of a newly established vine will usually aid in making it a more attractive specimen in later life.

Vines which climb by tendrils need a wire or string for support, and growth can be directed quite easily. The tendrils wrap around any slender object close enough to contact.

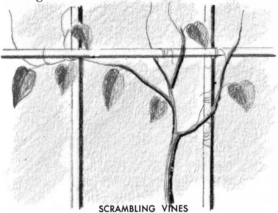

SCRAMBLING VINES

Vines with aerial rootlets or discs, to be grown on masonry or stucco walls, will soon "take hold." A small tack and tie in mortar joints will serve as a temporary anchor.

VINE SELF-SUPPORTING BY ROOTLETS

Vines and Ground Covers (Continued)

Twining vines twist as they grow, some clockwise, others counter-clockwise. If started in the natural direction of rotation, growth will be more rapid.

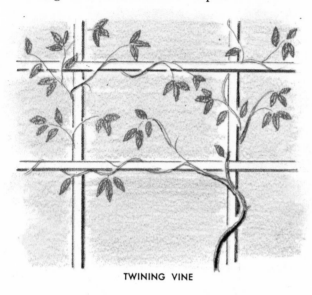

TWINING VINE

Scrambling vines, or scandent shrubs being used as vines need support against which to lean and must be tied to keep them in place. Use soft cord or special ties made for the purpose. Remember to keep ties loose to avoid constriction.

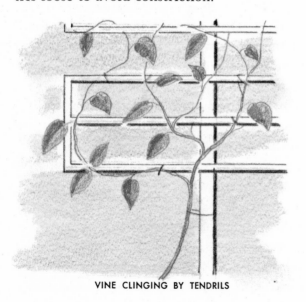

VINE CLINGING BY TENDRILS

PRUNING OF VINES

Some of the very vigorous vines can get out of hand quickly, so it is advisable to pinch out unwanted shoots and to cut back side branches regularly. If further control is needed, root pruning will usually suffice. If such vines are kept under control from the start, results will be much more pleasing. Train stems into place and do not allow them to cross or become entangled. Later care in removing old shoots and training new ones will be considerably less difficult.

As mentioned earlier, there are many families of plants represented among the vines so the pruning, and even the care of individuals, may vary considerably. Generally, the non-flowering vines may be pruned lightly at any time, or severely, when necessary, in late winter. Many of the flowering vines require special consideration in pruning because some bloom on new wood and can be pruned in winter, while others bloom from the old and prefer attention immediately after flowering. To get the most in beauty or utility from any vine, one should get to know it and its habits.

PEST CONTROL

Fortunately, vines as a class seem to be somewhat less susceptible to attack by insects and diseases than other plants. But it is also true that an infestation on a vine may be much more difficult to combat. For that reason, it is wise to start corrective measures just as soon as any unwelcome "guests" are detected.

Vines and Ground Covers *(Continued)*

Ground Covers

Ground covers, in the language of landscaping, have come to mean the many and diverse types of plants which are generally low-growing and of spreading habit and which may be used in a variety of landscape situations.

Ground covers may be used as lawn substitutes or to cover areas of bare ground. They often provide the solution to converting a problem spot in the garden to one of lasting beauty. Rough or otherwise hard-to-handle areas adjacent to lawns, heavily shaded areas where turf would fail, or dry sun-baked banks where it would be impossible to grow turf of any kind, are all examples of such problem areas. Wide variations in colors and textures allow a great deal of latitude in producing special landscape effects or of providing interesting tie-ins with the foundation planting. Then, too, it is possible to complement the type of architecture and setting in a more pleasing way. From the owner's viewpoint, ground covers make a welcome part of his planting because they practically eliminate the necessity for constant care in watering and mowing.

With all these benefits being offered, it is easy to understand why landscape men and gardeners are critically eyeing every plant which might be used to serve the above purposes. Many, in fact, feel that a ground cover in one form or another is an almost essential part of every landscape plan.

The variety of plants one may now see serving as ground covers grows larger every day. And since it includes a wide choice of woody deciduous as well as evergreen plants, vines, perennials and even succulents, there is no common denominator for planting and care. The ground cover must be fitted to the need, and selected with its suitability to existing cultural conditions in mind.

GROUND COVER TYPES

Extremely popular for areas where a flat and rather even effect is desired are such plants as wild strawberry, *Fragaria chiloensis,* or any of several ivy varieties. Generally, these present a satisfactory year around appearance, and maintenance is not a constant problem. Color and texture may be varied considerably by variety.

Great variations in foliage patterns, in color, both of foliage and flowers, habit of growth, and climatic adaptability, may be found among the many ground covers of more or less uneven habit, which grow in a "clumpy" or undulating manner.

There are types suitable as bank covers or for use around rocks, such as the prostrate junipers or low-growing *Cotoneaster dammeri.* For a relatively dry place, where moisture retention is difficult, *Ceanothus gloriosus* is a good bet. Bright, colorful flowers over a long season can be had with a planting of ivy geranium. Very cold-hardy yet evergreen are *Arctostaphylos uva-ursi* or *Lonicera halliana,* while *Vinca major* will grow in complete shade. Among the vines which make attractive ground covers are such favorites as *Hedera helix* or *Hedera canariensis, Trachelospermum jasminoides* and *Lonicera halliana.*

Vines and Ground Covers (Continued)

Culture

SOIL PREPARATION

Whether you are planting a ground cover or any other plant, good soil is important. Correcting deficiencies *before* planting can often save many times the cost in subsequent watering, fertilizing, and care. If the soil is too sandy, mixing a substantial amount of humus with it will lessen the job of keeping it moist and also will retard the leaching away of nutrients. Heavy clay soils are hard to till, become waterlogged easily, and often pack so tightly that plants are root-damaged by lack of aeration. Applying lime or gypsum, or working one of the new chemical flocculents into them, are ways of improving difficult clay or adobe soils.

While it is not a hard and fast rule, soils in the more arid sections are generally alkaline in reaction and low in humus. Those in sections where rainfall is heavy are apt to be acid in reaction.

As mentioned earlier, plants being used as ground covers represent a good many families and species and each has its own preference with respect to pH, moisture, or any other of the factors which can be considered as soil properties. Unless specifically mentioned in the description of the individual variety, it is probable that the plants will do reasonably well in any good soil, whether they are being used as ground covers or otherwise. However, when one is growing a ground cover, there can be a good deal of urgency because the sooner a solid mat is formed the sooner one is rid of the problem of keeping the area weeded, and the soil open and moist. To this end, it pays to have growing conditions as favorable as possible. A mulch of peat moss among newly set-out plants will help to hold moisture, prevent baking, and discourage weeds.

PLANTING GROUND COVERS

For economy's sake, those plants set out to ultimately make a solid mat, substituting for turf, are usually planted from so-called "flats" about 18 x 18 inches, which contain from 50 to 100 small plants of transplantable size. After the rows of plants have been "blocked out", as in the illustration below, rap the edge of the flat once or twice against a hard surface to loosen the soil from the bottom and to separate the soil from one edge to give you a starting place. It is then a simple matter to remove the individual plants with a paint or putty knife.

Vines and Ground Covers (Continued)

In planting these young plants from flats, it is well to keep the following points in mind:

1. Do your transplanting on a cool, cloudy day, or in the late afternoon. Young plants, especially those with larger foliage, suffer considerably if set out when it is hot and dry.

2. Do not select the largest plants available. These are too often overgrown and suffer more in transplanting than smaller ones, having less of a root system to disturb.

The spacing of plants set out from flats may vary considerably, depending upon the planter's anxiety to gain immediate effect as opposed to delayed coverage dictated by his finances. However, the general practice seems to be a spacing of 8 to 18 inches, or up to 2 feet for large-leaved ivy.

It is often quite difficult to establish plants on extremely steep banks because of the problem of holding moisture and because of "wash-outs". One fairly successful method is to cover the bank with a generous layer of straw held in place with inexpensive wide-mesh, light-gauge chicken wire, which can be "staked" down. The plants are set through the mesh.

Some ground covers, particularly the vines, may be planted from the popular "gallon" containers or from clay pots. Some of these may have staked shoots two feet or more in length. When unstaked and spread over the ground, the shoots will often layer (grow roots where covered with a little soil). These plants will fill in fairly fast if planted as much as 3 to 4 feet apart.

Most of the foregoing has had to do with the planting of "solid" covers where rapid "fill-in" is wanted. In planting spreading junipers or other types, where each plant has definite form or character, one must consider the ultimate spread of the plant as indicated in the variety description. Spacing can then be determined by separating the plants by distances approximating the expected spread of the individual.

WATERING

It is extremely important to watch young plants carefully for the first few weeks to be certain that they have adequate water. It often takes only an hour or so of drying heat or wind to cause them to wilt and droop. Once established, the requirements of plants used as ground covers may be about the same as though the plants were used in any other way, and their demands are dependent upon the type of soil, the weather and the varieties' own moisture requirements.

Regardless of what plants you may be growing, it pays to water thoroughly and deeply at each irrigation — then irrigate less frequently.

PRUNING

The pruning requirements of ground covers will vary considerably by variety. For example, aside from broken or dead branches, prostrate junipers will require no pruning at all. Some of the intermediate types like *Cotoneaster microphylla* or *Pyracantha* 'Santa Cruz' will require some pruning and shaping each year to keep them in bounds. Ivy, honeysuckle or other fairly fast-growing vines will, in a matter

Vines and Ground Covers (Continued)

of a couple of years, become too thick and matted. Severely cutting back and thinning out is necessary, but the established plants put on growth rapidly and the effects of this severe treatment are very soon erased.

Grass substitutes like *Dichondra* or *Lippia* may be mowed like any turf grass, but will require it only occasionally. Plants as coarse as *Fragaria* (wild strawberry), should be mowed about once or twice annually to keep them compact and good looking. A rotary-type mower is excellent for this purpose, but the reel types will also do the job if the cutter bar can be set for a height of about 2 inches.

LS754

Bougainvillea spectabilis 'Crimson Lake'

Colorful, evergreen, twining vine which grows vigorously to about 20 feet, but which may be pruned or trained almost as desired. For most of the year, but particularly in mid-summer, the plant is transformed into a spectacle of brilliance by myriads of glowing crimson leaf bracts. Likes rich soil and full sun. Fine coastal vine. Hardy to about 28 degrees.

LS755

Clematis armandi
ARMAND CLEMATIS

Evergreen clematis prized for its large, glossy, dark green foliage and its showy flowers. Grows very rapidly to about 25 feet once established, but can be pruned or trained as desired. In April, clusters of snow-white, star-like flowers are displayed in profusion. Prefers good, well drained soil and partial shade in warm dry areas. Hardy to about 15 degrees.

LS756

LS759

Clematis 'Mrs. Cholmondeley'

The large-flowered European hybrids are the most spectacular of all clematis, with star-like flowers often as much as 6 inches in diameter. Most varieties start flowering in June or July and continue for several weeks. Generally, flowers are borne on new wood, so spring pruning may be as severe as desired. Rich soil and good drainage are preferred — also partial shade in warm dry areas. All varieties are hardy to below zero degrees. *Mrs. Cholmondeley* is typical of the large-flowered hybrids.

LS760

Clematis montana rubens
PINK ANEMONE CLEMATIS

Like *C. montana* in all respects, except that the new foliage carries tints of red and the flowers are rose-pink instead of white.

Clematis montana
ANEMONE CLEMATIS

Vigorous, fast-growing, deciduous vine to 25 feet, with large toothed leaves. In May and June displays many 2-inch, anemone-like, white flowers. Blooms are borne on old wood so the vine should be pruned accordingly. Needs good drainage. Hardy below zero.

LS761

Clematis 'Ville de Paris'   LS765

This is one of the European hybrids described on page 80-2. See Mrs. Cholmondeley.

Clematis 'Ramona'   2127

One of the Evergreen hybrids. See Mrs. Cholmondeley.

Clematis 'Nellie Moser'   2268

Another European hybrid. See Mrs. Cholmondeley for description.

Clytostoma callistegioides Syn. *Bignonia speciosa*   1858
LAVENDER TRUMPET VINE

Strong-growing evergreen vine, thickly covered with large, good-looking foliage. Will soon clamber over a fence or trellis, needing support only on a wall. In late spring and early summer sprays of big trumpet-like flowers of delicate violet are borne in profusion. Sun or part shade. Hardy to about 20 degrees.

LS767

Doxantha unguis-cati Syn. *Bignonia tweediana*
CATCLAW FUNNELCREEPER

Fast-growing, evergreen vine which will climb high, clinging tenaciously to almost any surface by means of its "claws." Dense, glossy foliage is studded in spring with huge, trumpet-like flowers of brilliant yellow. Grows easily almost anywhere. Prefers full sun and thrives on heat. Deciduous in coldest areas. Hardy to about zero degrees.

LS770

△ **Fatshedera lizei**
FATSHEDERA

Hybrid between the giant-leaved *Fatsia (Aralia)* and Irish Ivy. Makes a shrubby vine with dramatic, large, shiny-lobed leaves, giving it a decided "tropical" look. Tends to grow upright, but can be supported and trained almost as desired. Not particular as to soil and is at home indoors or out. Hardy to about 10 to 15 degrees.

LS768

Gelsemium sempervirens
CAROLINA JESSAMINE

Twining vine with slender shoots and shining, bright, evergreen foliage. It grows moderately fast to about 15 feet, displaying in spring countless small, fragrant, bell-shaped flowers of golden yellow. Grows well in nearly all soils and climates. Hardy to about 15 degrees.

LS757

Hydrangea petiolaris
CLIMBING HYDRANGEA

Makes a large, robust, self-clinging vine, but may be kept to 10 or 15 feet by pruning. In June and July the dark green, heart-shaped leaves become a foil for the showy, big, 10-inch clusters of hydrangea-like flowers. Grows in sun or shade. Deciduous, and hardy below zero degrees.

947

⌂ Hibbertia volubilis
TWINING BUTTONFLOWER

Handsome vine of moderate size (10 or 12 feet) with dense, dark green, all-year foliage. For many weeks in late summer the vine is adorned with rose-like single flowers of shining clear yellow. Sun or part shade. Hardy to about 22 degrees.

LS758

Jasminum mesnyi Syn. *J. primulinum*
PRIMROSE JASMINE

Not a climber, but the long, green, pendulous branches may be trained easily over a fence or arbor. Often they are anchored at a height of 6 or 8 feet and allowed to cascade, fountain-like. In late winter, February to April, carries masses of gay yellow flowers. Easily grown almost anywhere. Hardy to about 15 degrees.

Passiflora alato-caerulea LS 762
PASSION FLOWER

Vigorous evergreen vine with soft green leaves which climbs rapidly by tendrils to 25 feet or more. During the entire summer there is a succession of the big 4 inch, strangely imbricated flowers. The outer petals are glistening white, flushed with pink, and frame a lacy crown of deep blue or purple. Sun or part shade. Hardy to about 24 degrees.

Phaedranthus buccinatorius Syn. *Bignonia chereri* 734
MEXICAN BLOOD TRUMPET

A large, strong-growing vine climbing by means of tendrils and covering large areas with a mantle of heavy, dark green foliage. Throughout most of the year bursts of bloom follow one another with the individual flowers varying from yellow at the base to rich red or purple at the lip. Grows best in the coastal belt in full sun. Hardy to about 24 degrees.

Polygonum auberti LS763
SILVER FLEECE VINE

Graceful, semi-deciduous vine, excellent for fast effect or quick overhead shade. Will grow 25 feet or more in a single season. New leaves are bronzy-red, turning to light green. In late spring and again in the fall the plant becomes a mass of very fragrant, little greenish-white flowers which hang in slender 6- to 8-inch panicles. Grows easily almost anywhere. Hardy to about 5 degrees.

Lonicera japonica halliana LS764
HALL'S JAPANESE HONEYSUCKLE

The common evergreen honeysuckle, well known everywhere and widely planted for its fast growth, dense foliage, and quantities of fragrant, creamy-white to yellow flowers. Grows readily in almost any soil; sun or shade. Often used as an aggressive ground cover. Hardy to about 5 degrees.

2502

Trachelospermum jasminoides
STAR JASMINE

A twining, fast-growing vine, climbing with support to 30 feet or so. Will quickly cover a fence, trellis or pergola. Can be trained as a ground cover by pinching back to produce horizontal growth. All summer long the branches are tipped with clusters of jasmine-scented, 1-inch flowers of snowy white. Easily grown, sun or part shade. Hardy to about 5 degrees but is semi-deciduous.

LS766

LS545

Trachelospermum fragrans
JASMINE

Scandant evergreen shrub or woody small vine with abundant, dark green, leathery leaves. For many weeks in summer snowy-white, 1-inch flowers in clusters of three will scent the garden with typical jasmine fragrance. Sun or part shade. Hardy to about 20 degrees.

Wisteria floribunda
JAPANESE WISTERIA

Strong-growing and long-lived, deciduous vine, which will ultimately cover a huge area. Before leaves appear in spring, the entire plant is decked out in long, pendulous clusters of violet blue, sweetpea-like flowers, filling the garden with fragrance. Plant in full sun. Hardy to about 5 degrees above zero.

LS769

2246

Wisteria sinensis
CHINESE WISTERIA

Large, woody, deciduous vine growing to 50 feet or more but usually tailored by pruning to fit into a desired space or shape. This never fails to become a mass of pendant, violet-blue flower clusters each spring, just before the leaves appear. Full sun. Hardy to about 10 degrees.

2247

⌂ Wisteria floribunda 'Rosea'
PINK JAPANESE WISTERIA

Like the Chinese Wisteria in size and growth characteristics but somewhat more airy and less densely foliaged. The marked difference is in the remarkable length of these flower clusters. The slender racemes of light lavender-pink blooms of this variety may be as much as 3 feet in length. Easily grown in full sun. Hardy to about 5 degrees.

Wisteria floribunda violaceo-plena
DOUBLE VIOLET JAPANESE WISTERIA

Similar to Wisteria floribunda 'Rosea,' except that the flowers in the long racemes are double, violet in color, and very fragrant.

LS779

Arctostaphylos uva-ursi
BEARBERRY

Trailing evergreen shrub with small, glossy, green leaves. Spreads to 10 feet or more once established and is excellent for use in a rock garden or for covering a sandy slope. In late spring carries clusters of small, pink-tinged, white flowers which are later followed by bright red fruits. Needs sun, rather dry soil, and perfect drainage. Hardy to 30 or 40 degrees below zero.

Cotoneaster microphylla
ROCKSPRAY COTONEASTER

Small-leaved evergreen cotoneaster which may grow to 2 feet tall but will spread to considerably more, the long runners often rooting. Planted 3 to 4 feet apart, the plants will make a dense blanket of dark green foliage. White spring flowers, followed by red berries in fall. Sun or shade. Hardy about zero degrees.

LS780

LS781

Cotoneaster dammeri
BEARBERRY COTONEASTER

Most prostrate of the cotoneasters, an irregular, sprawling, woody plant, useful for rocky slopes, or effective cascading over a wall. Has small, shiny green foliage and white flowers in spring, followed by bright red berries in fall. Prefers sun, not too much water. Hardy to about 10 degrees.

Ceanothus gloriosus
POINT REYES CEANOTHUS

Makes a dense, undulating, evergreen mat, varying in height from 6 to 10 inches and spreading to 6 feet or more. In late spring a profusion of fragrant, little, lavender-blue flowers appear in small, rounded clusters. Needs good, well-drained soil but will take more water than other ceanothus. Hardy to about 10 degrees.

Juniperus sabina 'Tamariscifolia'
SPREADING SAVIN JUNIPER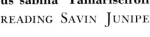

One of the best of the junipers where a low spreading type is needed. Makes a complete mound of grey-green foliage, spreading its irregular, pointed branches to 10 feet or more. Seldom exceeds 18 inches in height. Grows readily in most any soil or climate. Full sun. Hardy to zero degrees.

Juniperus sabina
SAVIN JUNIPER

A thickly-foliaged shrub of deep green spreading in a rather stiff manner. Quite variable, but generally under 6 feet in height. May spread to 12 feet or more. Leaves and branches give off a strong aromatic odor when bruised. Easily grown, and hardy to about 25 degrees below zero.

Fragaria chiloensis
CHILOE STRAWBERRY

Plants spread rapidly by runners to make a thick, low, mat of lush, dark green foliage. An occasional bright red leaf adds interest. One-inch, white flowers in spring precede small, edible, bright red strawberries. An occasional "high" mowing will help to keep it neat. Needs plenty of moisture. Hardy to about 10 degrees.

LS783

2368

LS782

Erica darleyensis
DARLEY HEATH

An evergreen shrub thriving in acid soils forming a "porcupine" bush of 8 to 15 inches in height and 2 to 3 feet in width. Spreading habit requires pruning annually to retain its clump form. Bright red flowers from January through May. Hardy to about 10 degrees below zero.

LS784

Hypericum calycinum
AARONSBEARD; ROSE OF SHARON

Low evergreen shrub 10 to 12 inches tall, spreading by means of underground runners. Plants set out 12 to 18 inches apart will rapidly fill in to make a compact mat of attractive green foliage. In summer carries a profusion of bright yellow, 3-inch flowers. Sun or part shade. Hardy to about 10 degrees.

LS785

Hedera helix
ENGLISH IVY

Well known evergreen vine with dark, glossy, 3-inch leaves. Will grow moderately fast, clinging to a wall, fence or trellis by means of aerial rootlets. Ivy is used in many ways, even as a ground cover, and is popular because of its year-around good looks. Grows readily almost everywhere. Hardy to about 10 degrees or lower in some forms such as *baltica*.

Planting of ground covers:

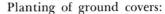 **Hedera helix,** English Ivy (on bank) with
Pelargonium lateripes
    (*P. hederaefolium; P. peltatum lateripes*)

IVYLEAF PELARGONIUM OR
IVYLEAF GERANIUM

LS264

Ceanothus gloriosus
Point Reyes Ceanothus
See page 80-10 for description

Juniperus sabina 'Tamariscifolia'
Spreading Savin Juniper
See page 80-10 for description

Hedera canariensis
Canary Island Ivy

Of the many varieties of Ivy, those of the species *H. canariensis* are most commonly used as ground covers in warm climates because they thrive in sun and heat. An evergreen, woody vine with large, angular, 3- to 5-lobed leaves. Requires spring pruning to keep neat and in bounds. Hardy to about 10 degrees above zero.

LS787

Pyracantha crenato-serrata 'Santa Cruz'

A dense, prostrate form of pyracantha seldom over 18 inches in height, but may spread irregularly to 6 feet or more. Has handsome, glossy, dark green, all-year foliage, white flowers in spring and clusters of big, showy, scarlet berries in late fall and winter. Sun or part shade. Hardy to about 15 degrees.

LS312

Vinca minor
Common Periwinkle

Evergreen vine or trailer, particularly useful as a ground or bank cover. Grows easily almost anywhere and will even thrive in full shade. Almost as soon as growth starts, flowers appear and continue to open until frost. They are about one inch across and may be blue, white or purple by variety. Hardy to about 15 degrees below zero.

LS786

GARDEN PLANTS IN COLOR

Index

Bold face type indicates the approved scientific name.
Small Capitals indicate approved horticultural variety and common names.
Italic type denotes synonyms.